In Health, On Purpose!

Awakening Your True Calling in the Healthcare Profession

•••••••• *Nicole Thomas*, MSN, RN, CCM ••••••

In Health, on Purpose! Awakening Your True Calling in the Healthcare Profession
Copyright© 2016
Published by Nicole Thomas Enterprises
ISBN: 978-0-99843282-0-7

Scripture taken from the New King James Version® Copyright© 1982 by Thomas Nelson. Used by permission. All rights reserved.

Cover Design and Content Editing: Brown & Duncan Brand, LLC.

Cover Photographer: Christopher Horne

Dedication

This book is dedicated to a man who helped me understand what it truly means to live and not merely exist, my stepfather, James Willie Millsap; my extremely supportive and "ride or die" husband, Edward Thomas; my daughters, Diamond Bailey and Emily Thomas; my supportive mother, Helen Millsap, and a host of family and friends.

Table Of Contents

Introduction:
You Are on Assignment

Living a purpose-filled life means that you are living each day in the assignment God has designed for you. This assignment should be your passion — it makes you whole and completes you. When you are living in purpose, you are living on purpose as well. This means you are intentional about the decisions you make, how you spend your time, and pursuing your assignment. You don't just accept anything offered to you. You are intentional and deliberate. You know exactly why you are here and the groups that you are called to serve.

As professionals in the healthcare industry, we have a special calling on our lives to make a difference in an area that is close to God's heart and important for his kingdom — health and healing. God has called us to serve his children who are plagued with sickness and disease in their minds and bodies. Every day, we are used as vessels to carry out a mission that demonstrates his power on earth. Healthcare is our profession, and while we may be employed by independent physician practices, hospitals, pharmacies, nursing homes or urgent care facilities, the one who determines our destiny — who has truly employed us — is God.

1

He is our boss. It is our duty to learn what healthcare ministry He has called us to and where we belong. As a former medical-surgical and managed care nurse, and current consultant in the healthcare field, I have met many healthcare professionals who were anything but intentional when they selected their careers. Many people chose nursing or healthcare in general because of the money, the ability to earn a decent living without a lot of schooling, and the flexible hours. I can't explain how problematic this thinking is. I've also met many nurses who are just plain confused. They are not happy, and you can tell they aren't passionate about their careers. I believe this is because they are misplaced within the field. At some point, they probably had a desire to help people and to serve those who were sick or hospitalized. But then, their voices were silenced. They were put in positions that didn't fit their desires, and they began to simply live rather than thrive. If any of these scenarios describe you, we are going to address that too. This book will help you identify your true calling, tap into your passion and jump back on the road that leads to your true purpose. When we live on purpose, we will make a true impact in the field.

> *"Before I formed you in the womb I knew you;*
> *Before you were born I sanctified you;*
> *I ordained you a prophet to the nations."*
> **Jeremiah 1:5**

My goal is that as a result of reading this book, you will understand without a doubt that God designed a unique purpose for you in the healthcare field. Most importantly, my goal is to inspire and encourage you to discover your purpose in this field and become determined to manifest and walk in it wholeheartedly. Too often, healthcare professionals have been lied to. We have been made to believe that we are supposed to fade into the background, be quiet and simply serve as support to others' ideas and missions. But that couldn't be further from the truth. Nurses, radiologists, phlebotomists et al. are innovators, encouragers, creators, and I want you to be bold and courageous in your calling. Everyone is not called to healthcare, but to those who are called, it is important for us to walk boldly in our purpose, and so we first have to discover it!

We have much work to do! Below is a checklist of what is to come, and it's going to serve as your GPS through this book.

Through *In Health, On Purpose! Awakening Your True Calling in the Healthcare Profession*, you will:

- Uncover how to truly define purpose

- Begin action-oriented strategies to assist you with determining your purpose as a healthcare professional

- Discuss the consequences of losing sight of that purpose

- Review the action steps to regain control of your purpose

- Learn how to live in your purpose to make an impact on the healthcare industry

- Learn to leave your mark as a healthcare professional

In Health, On Purpose!

Chapter 1:
What Defines True Purpose?

      Purpose … a simple, yet powerful word. This word has so many definitions, perspectives and opinions depending on whom you ask. According to Webster, *purpose is the reason for which something is done and created or for which something exists.* Bishop T.D. Jakes, an American pastor and bishop of The Potter's House, author, filmmaker and my mentor (in my head), defines purpose as *"an underlying chemistry that makes you live your life."* According to the best-selling book of all time, the Holy Bible, our purpose is the reason we are here, and every believer has a purpose that is rooted in God's plan for the earth and His sovereign will. Isaiah 43:7 (ESV) says *"Everyone who is called by my name, whom I created for my glory, whom I formed and made…"*

      As you can see there are several different perspectives about the definition of purpose. As a woman of faith and healthcare consultant to other faith-filled professionals and purpose-driven business owners, I believe that God created us to match perfectly with a purpose designed for our individual lives. This goes for healthcare professionals

5

as well. I needed to write this book especially for the nurse who has lost her passion, the single-mother who works 16-hour shifts in the hospital to find that it's still not enough, and the medical student who is facing challenges that she did not bargain for. Don't give up. Your purpose is waiting for you.

Have you ever asked yourself questions like: *How can I determine my true purpose? What am I here for? Is my talent my purpose? How am I going to know what my purpose is? When will I know for sure?* ... Most likely if you are still reading this book, you have. Trying to figure out our purpose in life causes us stress and sleepless nights. We worry that we are not living in our purpose and that we've missed it altogether, but the reality is that discovering our purpose is not an overnight thing. Most people want to go to bed and wake up the next day and know, "Oh this is my purpose!" Sorry, it does not work like that. The journey to purpose is a long process that causes so many different emotions, including frustration, defeat, feelings of useless-ness and disappointment. In fact, figuring out my own purpose has been one of the hardest experiences I have had to *endure* in my life.

Let me tell you, I am a woman of many talents. I am talented at organizing parties and events for my family and friends. At one point, I questioned whether my purpose was to be a party planner. I also love decorating spaces within my home. People often walk into my house, fall in love with the interior decorating, and they immediately try to get me to redecorate their homes as well. I am so good at this that I use to wonder whether I should become an interior decorator. I can clean a house spic and span, to the point where you can literally see your reflection on my floor. And yes, I asked myself if I should become a professional cleaner, too. I often find myself teaching people about health sciences and I enjoy teaching the ins and outs of our complex body system, and making it simple enough for a fifth grader to understand how the body works. With a skill like that, surely I could have become an elementary school science or biology teacher right? I can go on and on about the various gifts that I have. If I were desperate for cash, I would be able to put any of these talents to use. I am so talented that I have no problem declaring, "I will never be broke!" However, I had to soon learn that just because I am good at so many things, it did not mean they are my true purpose in life. So I had to pump the brakes (meaning put a stop to all of my activity, *immediately*).

With all of the talents that you possess, discovering your purpose within this life should be easy, right? Ha! As I think back on my journey, I laugh because all of my talents didn't make discovering my purpose any easier. Unfortunately, just the opposite is true. Your talent may not be your purpose. Just think about how many things you are great at, the things you can do with your eyes closed. How many skills have you learned throughout your life? And you may be wondering *what's the purpose of even having so much talent if I am not called to do these things permanently...*if they are not your purpose? In life, we often start off working and performing in our talents. We may even accept a few jobs based on a skill we have learned or something we enjoy doing, only to find that we still feel unfulfilled. This is because our talents are not necessarily our purpose. What happens more often is that our talents and skills are stops on a road that leads us to our purpose. Every stop leads to the next and the next until eventually, we realize we know exactly what we've been designed to do. This is especially true in the healthcare field. As a healthcare professional, my journey to purpose, for instance, was less about determining and more about awakening.

There are generally three types of purpose-seekers: Those whose purpose came easily to them. Maybe they "just knew" what they were supposed to do. There's a second group of people who find the process of discovering purpose to be very complex. These types of people try many different things until it finally clicks. The third group of people finds this to be a terrifying process. They may be confused or simply paralyzed by the fear of their purpose.

Why is the journey toward a purpose-filled life so different for everyone? I've learned that the people who find it difficult to determine their true purpose have not tapped into the source yet. They are not plugged into the outlet. They are not tuned into the correct channel, and that source, outlet, and channel is God. People who walk in fear that they will live an unfulfilling life that lacks purpose *forever* are often afraid of change. Sometimes they are fearful because they know that their purpose is getting ready to shake up something serious in their lives and that their *own* human desires are about to go out of the window if they don't align with God's will. When you walk in TRUE purpose, your life is officially no longer about you. Remember Isaiah 43:7: *God formed everyone that he has called for his glory…* and Jeremiah 1:5: *before God formed you, he knew you and sanctified you (ordained you)…* Those who don't have an issue discovering and living in their true purpose surrender to God's will and admit, "Lord I don't know what's best for me, please take over and drive the wheel."

Let's reflect back on the three types of purpose seekers: Remember the person who had no problem at all discovering his/her purpose? Identify someone like this in your own life — a friend or family member who has always been intentional, content and able to make an impact in what they do on a day-to-day basis. Find out what has enabled this person to live such a purpose-filled life. Figure out what has driven and sustained them — you may find that it has been his/her faith!

Let's just cut to the chase and call a thing a thing here. Determining your true purpose as a healthcare professional is not an easy thing. But we as humans often make it more complicated than it really has to be. Do we put more into discovering our purpose than what it actually is? Do we often operate in our will rather than the will of God? The answer is a simply YES! We as fleshy people want to say well, "God gave me this talent, so it is my purpose" or "It feels good to me, and I can do it easily" or maybe we tell ourselves, "I can imagine a life doing this! It must be my purpose." And we often think, "I am comfortable with it, so this *is obviously* my purpose." But the truth is that to determine your true purpose as a healthcare professional, and I repeat to determine YOUR TRUE PURPOSE, you must submit and surrender to God ... point ... blank ... period ...! There is no way around this step, and there is no one you can call for a hook-up to help you to figure this out. There is no amount of money that will make "purpose" be mailed to you by UPS. You can enroll in as many online courses and attend as many seminars as you want, but if you do not start with this first step (submission), you will be paying "coaches" forever to help you figure it out. You must surrender to the creator for He is the only one who knows exactly why He put you here on this earth and gave you this assignment in the healthcare industry.

Do not stop at where you are comfortable. Do not stop seeking purpose because you make loads of money or because you *feel* that you have reached a certain level of success in life as a healthcare provider. If you are unfulfilled and you know that you are not living in your purpose and on purpose, you should seek first the kingdom of God, so that He can add everything else that you need to your life, and prune you of what no longer belongs. Many people stop searching and seeking purpose, simply because they feel they are already "successful." They stop seeking once they have reached these temporary stops in the journey as if these places — and material gains — were the final destination. Anything short of your purpose is simply transportation to your destination and your life's true purpose.

Chapter 2:

Discovering Your Purpose in Healthcare

• •

"If you can't figure out your purpose, figure out your passion. For your passion will lead you right into your purpose." — Bishop T.D. Jakes

The average person who decides to enter the health-care industry does so because they "want to help people." This is absolutely honorable because we are all placed here to serve, but what exactly does "help people" mean? The truth is that you can work in many other professions, be-sides healthcare, and still help people. Think about it: The auto repairman helps people fix their cars, the personal shopper helps people look fashionable, the hair stylist helps women look and feel glamorous. I can go on and on about the various jobs and professions where we can "help" people. But what makes healthcare professionals different? Are we simply helping people just like everyone else who "helps" people or are we set apart? I'm convinced that our purpose should indeed set us apart. You may be working in your purpose as a healthcare professional. Maybe you considered your calling prior to entering this field, and you indeed followed your passion. Perhaps you received a rev-

11

elation from God, and He told you exactly what you were put here to do. However, I find that more often than not, healthcare professionals simply follow their yearning to "help" people versus matching their desire to make a difference with their talents, interests, lifestyles and instructions they received from the Holy Spirit through prayer.

In the previous chapter, we went pretty deep on this thing called purpose as it relates to defining or determining what you are truly called to do. I want you to take a moment to decide if you have a different outlook on your own career after reading the first chapter of this book. Are you truly destined to be a healthcare professional?

The short quiz that follows will allow you to evaluate if you are purposed to be in the healthcare profession:

1. Are you excited to wake up for work each morning despite the barriers that you know the day will bring? Why or why not?

_____

_____

_____

_____

_____

_____

_____

_____

_____

_____

_____

2. What else could you imagine yourself doing if you were not in the healthcare industry?

_____

_____

_____

_____

_____

_____

_____

_____

_____

_____

3. Do you ever regret choosing this career path? Why or why not?

_____

_____

_____

_____

_____

_____

_____

_____

_____

_____

_____

4. If you were furloughed (without pay) for three months, would you remain in your current position, look for a similar position with a different company or rethink your career?

_____

_____

_____

_____

_____

_____

_____

_____

_____

_____

_____

5. In the previous question, if you decided that you would look for a similar position with a different company or rethink your career, why do you want to do this?

_____

_____

_____

_____

_____

_____

_____

_____

_____

_____

_____

Review your answers to those questions to determine if there is an underlying theme of happiness and satisfaction or discontent and unhappiness within your career. You may have realized that you are in the right field. If so, that's great! I want you to continue reading. If the questions above prompt you to have a different outlook on what you are doing, then that is OK as well. My suggestion for you would be to take out a piece of paper, separate it into two columns, and in one column list your passions and the next column list your talents. Seek God's guidance through prayer. Be very sensitive to where God is leading you as you begin to brainstorm on a field that will enable you to operate within your passion points.

Awakening to your true purpose is not an overnight process, and most people go through many jobs, and sometimes professions, before they awaken to their true purpose. It is a process of trial and error — when passion meets talent and prayer reveals truth.

Awakening to Purpose

I say that discovering our purpose is an "awakening" process because once you know what you were created for, a new world with new perspectives opens up to you. It is as if the blindfold has been lifted. These perspectives are not available while you are still unaware of (and asleep to) your purpose. You truly are sleeping, and unfortunately for those who try to take short cuts, who refuse to submit as we discussed in the previous chapter, they will remain blinded to their true purpose.

In Chapter 1, I spoke about the spiritual implications behind discovering purpose. Our life is not our own, and we must be awakened to Christ before we can do what we were truly put on this earth to do. We may be walking on our purpose path, helping people or acquiring skills and tools

15

that will help us in our true calling, *long* before we come to know Jesus. But when we submit to Him and make Him Lord over our lives, He makes everything we have done before Him all make sense. For instance, you may have always been a nurturer. Perhaps you have had to take care of elderly relatives while you were growing up or raise your younger siblings. Then in high school, you found yourself volunteering at a local nursing home, day care or shelter. You may have always been doing work in the field that you are called to. It was your passion before. But once you allow Jesus in your heart and ask Him to show you the way, He will connect all of the dots and, in hindsight, you will see how each stop in your journey made you who you were called to be. You will find yourself at that destination called "purpose." Or even better than that, let me use myself as an example. I have always been an advice giver, a person who is always explaining to someone how to perform a task or complete an action. I am a person who likes to lead the pack. My closest and dearest family and friends also know I have a love for the functionality of the human body and the science surrounding it.

This passion led me to pursuing a career in the healthcare profession as a nurse. I naturally gravitated toward a field that allowed me to give advice, help others, be a leader and share information about the human anatomy and how our bodies work. These elements combined have placed me in positions where I served as a director of managed care for a Fortune 500 company, a nurse educator and consultant, but it wasn't until I surrendered my own will and allowed God into my heart that He connected all of the dots and took me on a journey to my purpose as a healthcare professional. Not until you are willing to connect to the source, will you truly understand your purpose. When you connect to the source, you will be awakened to new possibilities. God will make it all make sense for you.

In Health, On Purpose!

After working through the above exercise, you should know if healthcare is your purpose. The following section is for those of you who, without a doubt, are called into the healthcare industry. Let's dig below the surface a bit. To reiterate, some people enter the field simply because they want to help people. They may take the path of least resistance in order to get their foot in the door, but fail to turn on the navigation system once they are in. So instead of making U-turns or exits when they realize a position just isn't quite right, they continue traveling down that same path until they look up after years and realize they are not doing what they love or was destined to do.

Sometimes, when they look up, they realize that they have traveled so far in the wrong direction that they are not sure where they even steered off course from the main high-way that leads to their true purpose. Whether you can relate to this or you simply want to discover your purpose and learn the options available to you, the following discussion can serve as your starting point. Let's carve out your niche in this field.

So, what is my purpose as a healthcare professional?

The stakes of our industry are life and death. With that said, it's important that each of us realize who and what we are. It is important that we are also passionate and intentional about what we do. There are various positions in this industry and several duties and assignments that can fall under a given title. You have various options available to you, depending on your interests and experiences. For example, you may be a nurse and have the gift of IV insertion. You might become well-known throughout your hospital for your ability to insert IVs painlessly. No matter if a patient has rolling veins, disappearing veins or hiding veins … regardless the challenge a patient's veins present, and even when no other nurse can insert that IV, you can get it on the first or second try! That is your talent. But does that mean your purpose within healthcare is to be an infusion nurse? Let's consider another example: You are a Certified Nursing Assistant (CNA) and your talent as a CNA is making all of your patients feel like a new person after they complete a whirlpool bath because you give the best darn whirlpool baths. Does that mean your purpose in healthcare is to be the lead whirlpool operator? Or what about the radiology technician who has the talent to get the precise radiological images that she needs on the first take. Does that mean her purpose as a healthcare professional is to be the manager of the radiology department? Do you see where I am going here? One of my closest colleagues, Karen, has the gift of getting the MOST difficult patients to open up and answer deep personal health questions that NO one else can get them to be honest about, not even physicians.

Karen has a certain aura about her; she is so darn personable and relatable. Patients love her. So at my office, it is common knowledge that if anyone needs to know intimate details about a patient that only the patient can give us, we need to get Karen on that task because she will have no problems getting this info. Once she awakened to her purpose, Karen took this innate gift and opened a community healthcare resource center for the underserved and poverty-stricken population in Louisiana. Through various jobs, assignments, and stops along her purpose path, Karen awakened to her unique gift, and she understood that she had the ability to connect with almost anyone and make an impact on their lives. She is the perfect example of someone who is *in health on purpose!* As healthcare professionals, we have to first ensure that our purpose is to be in the healthcare field and then we have to go even deeper to determine what our true purpose is as healthcare professionals because every individual who is supposed to be in this industry has a specific purpose.

Unlimited Options

I realize that for many in the healthcare industry, the type of thinking discussed in this book is new and perhaps you have never considered whether or not you are in health on purpose. If this is true for you, my hope is that by reading many of the examples of others who are in health on purpose, you too will be exposed to new possibilities. Not everyone in our field touches patients, hospitals, IV machines and medicine. There are some people who also love to help people and make a difference, and their sole purpose is to fight for healthcare institutions, new laws and patients' rights on Capitol Hill. There are healthcare attorneys who protect institutions or those who fight for patients. They are advocates. Some individuals work in the field to educate communities on various issues in health, be it weight loss, cancer prevention or flu vaccinations. They may facilitate workshops and health fairs. Then we have health advocates who work in human resources departments of organizations to help employees select healthcare providers. Or they might evaluate various benefits to ensure their colleagues have health and wellness options available to them. Then you have some whose true purpose is to find cures for different diseases. They are our researchers. Other individuals have been called to care for the elderly, especially in their last days — these people not only care for patients but they also console families as well. You have activists who speak out against public health concerns such as AIDS, health implications of poverty, death, etc. There are so many opportunities to be in health on purpose and to help people while using healthcare as your tool.

Talents versus Purpose

Since I was a little girl with pigtails in elementary school, I have known that I was going to be a nurse. Honestly, I had this epiphany as a little girl. As I grew older, no matter how many times I was asked, "What are you going to be when you grow up?" and regardless of who was doing the asking, I would proudly say, "A nurse." Never an astronaut, President of the United States, a singer, America's Next Top Model or fashion designer or anything else that we fantasize about as children. Nope, I was going to grow up to become a nurse. So that is just what I did. After I graduated from high school, I immediately went to college to pursue nursing.

As a nurse, I had quite a few talents. I was one of those people who was gifted at getting difficult IV sticks in no more than two attempts. I am also great at managing a caseload of six patients, supervising a successful staff of diverse individuals, educating aspiring and new nurses, and the list goes on. With all of these talents that I had, was my purpose to become an infusion nurse, to be a manager, teach nurses…? Any of those areas could have been my fate because I knew that God anointed me to become a nurse — and a great one at that. But I had to dig deeper and realize that learning the variety of skills throughout my journey as a nurse were necessary to prepare me for what my true calling and purpose would be — a nurse's consultant, author, and purpose coach.

Do you see now how it is easier for me to identify with nurses whom I coach and consult with as someone who has been in their shoes before? My past experiences were also a huge benefit to the attorneys who were clients of my company Impact Nurse Consultants. As an insider in the healthcare industry, I could help them navigate their health-related cases. The experience I had as a manager, nurse educator, and director of managed care prepared me for the business side of healthcare, and I was able to take my passions, apply my talent and excel. This is what God destined me to do and every stop along the way built me and equipped me for my calling. Don't confuse your talents with your purpose because they are not the same. The former is just a vehicle to get you to the latter.

As we read in Chapter 1, defining your purpose is not an overnight task by any means. But as healthcare professionals, it seems as if we have it a little bit harder because we know we are supposed to be in the healthcare profession as a nurse, physician, certified nursing assistant, etc., but what is our actual purpose in this role? *Where do I fit in as a healthcare professional? How do I leave my mark so that people remember me when I'm gone like we do nursing pioneers Florence Nightingale or Mary Mahoney?*

These are some of the questions that we as healthcare providers will eventually face as we continue to work in this industry. We are called to make a difference, and God wants to reveal our true purpose so we do not wander around in circles by repeatedly doing what He has not designed for us. When you're living on purpose, you will have an impact and leave a legacy behind. It took me some time to realize that one of the main benefits of living in health on purpose is that we won't have to try hard to leave a mark. Our purpose was created for us with an internal default — to bring that purpose to past and to make an impact.

We often come into healthcare because we want to change lives and we jump in head first to save all of those who come our way. Then something starts to happen within us. We start to get an itch to experience other areas of healthcare, which is an excellent thing because there are so many areas of healthcare that needs us. We move from generalized direct patient care to a specialty, such as case management, critical care, oncology, pediatrics, mental health, education, and the list goes on and on. But after that move and working in that arena for quite some time, we inevitably want more. I have worked with countless healthcare professionals and we all seem to get the "itch" to do more. We may go back to school while we're working to gain new skills and sharpen our talents. No matter how many changes you make, do not get discouraged. Remember that each experience and every transition are simply vehicles that will provide new skills and talents that will be necessary when you arrive at your place of purpose.

Everyone in healthcare has a certain role that they are designed to fill. Everyone is not supposed to be the physician, the nurse, the community health advocate, the vice president of a health system, the radiologist, the direct care professional, the research expert, etc. I know there are people in healthcare, some of you reading this book, who are working in capacities that may not be the right fit for you and that is OK because you just need to zero in and determine your place as a healthcare professional. Refuse to allow your title to define who you are. Please do not become complacent.

I have noticed that many people in the healthcare field settle. Some of us should be the inventors of the machines we use, some of us are supposed to be the people who discover cures for AIDS and cancer. Some of us would be ideal on Capitol Hill fighting for health policies, and others were made to be healthcare entrepreneurs who create opportunities for others who have been called to purpose. It is virtually impossible to be a great leader when you are still trying to figure things out. It's important that healthcare professionals awaken to their purpose, walk in their purpose and THRIVE in their purpose! That is truly when we are able to help others walk in their purpose as well.

Decide What's Best for You
What are your talents as a healthcare professional?
What are you passionate about?

These are two questions that you should ask yourself as you try to determine where you belong within the health industry. Once you tap into your talents and passions, begin to work in them. Be diligent because one opportunity will lead to the next and the next until you find yourself doing exactly what God called you to do. Notice that you have to take the first step if you want to walk and work in your purpose. God is not going to just drop your purpose into your lap. He is waiting for you to become willing, available and ready to make a decision. Your first step is to simply DECIDE.

Once you decide to walk in purpose and take that first step, then God will reveal your purpose to you. Once He does, walk in it unapologetically. Be unapologetically aggressive and focused when it comes to your purpose. This is important because distractions will arise that will threaten your focus and your purpose walk. Everyone is not going to understand why you do what you do, act the way you act, say what you say, give how you give, and so forth. And that is OK because the purpose that God has for each of us is different and *they* don't have to understand *your purpose* because it is not for anyone to understand except you. I will never get why my mom, in her elder years, helps people to the point where her knees hurt, feet swell and her hands literally blister. I can't understand it at all. I sometimes try to get her to behave otherwise too, but guess what,

23

she never tries to explain *her purpose* to me anymore. She is walking in her purpose and doing exactly what God called her to do. As a healthcare consultant and nurse leader, I no longer try to explain to my fellow counterparts why I will work in my business and place of employment for eight to nine hours per day and then leave there to spend another two to three hours, three times per week mentoring aspiring nurses, novice nurses and other healthcare professionals to the point where my eyes literally burn from being so tired. I am walking in my purpose as an educator, motivator, and purposeful living enthusiast, so I don't really care or worry about family, friends and other colleagues who tell me, "Nicole you are doing too much," or ask me, "Why do you have to help everybody?" This is my purpose and it doesn't need any explanations. Yours doesn't either.

As a healthcare professional, you will have co-workers, family members, friends and neighbors who question your decisions: "What are you doing, a Nurse Practitioner is not supposed to be doing this?" Or they may say that a Certified Nursing Assistant is *supposed* to assist patients with their activities of daily living, *not* host community forums to educate caregivers. So many people have asked me, "Wait, you are a nurse, so why don't you work in a hospital or physician's office? What do you mean that you are a "nursepreneur"? What kind of business are you doing because most nurses work in hospitals and wear scrubs." Whenever I get hounded like that, I politely laugh and say, "I am a nurse that lives on purpose."

That's all I say because it is my God-given purpose and *my* journey, so I am not going to explain to anyone or try to make them understand why I am not doing things the way others have always done them. I am not being mean or rude, but I have learned that when you walk in purpose, you don't have to explain yourself to anyone! Be unapologetically you, and in healthcare, be on purpose.

Chapter 3:

Have You Lost Sight of Your Purpose in Healthcare?

• •

Two of the worst things that can happen to a health-care professional are not determining your purpose or losing sight of it. Either of these two situations will eventually lead to feelings of depression, anxiety, frustration, doubt, burnout and alienation. Oftentimes, these feelings lead to healthcare professionals totally walking away from the profession because they have not put in the work to determine where they fit. Too many of our colleagues have allowed the "industry" to dampen their spirits. The increasing demands that are being placed on healthcare providers, politics and laws that affect the healthcare industry, staffing issues and emotional stress all add up, leading to burnout and disappointment for many.

As I mentioned, I am a "nursepreneur," and so I am always on the prowl for new data and facts that reveal trends about my industry. The results from a recent study by the American Association of Colleges of Nursing was disheartening to me as a nurse. It indicated that by 2025 the nursing profession will experience a shortage of 500,000

27

nurses and it is estimated that 30-50 percent of all new registered nurses will change their positions or completely leave the healthcare industry. According to an article published by *Forbes* magazine, 45 percent of physicians said that they are contemplating leaving the profession early because they are fed-up with the politics that prevent them from providing the proper care needed to adequately care for their patients. The Associated Third Party Administrators (ATPA) projects that by the year 2020 there will be a shortage of approximately 41,000 allied healthcare professionals, which is largely contributed to an attrition rate of 3.5 percent of allied health workers. Now in case you are wondering why this is so significant, allied health professionals are responsible for transcribing diagnostic studies. They also rehab patients in their roles as physical, occupation, speech and respiratory therapists, and they perform medical sonograms. They make provision of dietary and nutrition services, apply scientific principles and evidence-based practices so that patient outcomes can be optimized, and many other things. They make up 60 percent of the healthcare profession and are a critical component of the medical industry. If the attrition rate continues at this current rate, the healthcare profession will be in a state of crisis. These alarming numbers represent a red flag for our industry. People in healthcare are losing their passion and are not operating on purpose.

Despite these alarming statistics, these numbers could be significantly diminished if we as healthcare professionals were truly plugged into the source (God) that placed us here in the healthcare profession. So many healthcare professionals are "scientists" and if you are familiar with the everlasting debate surrounding an existence of God, you know that many atheists do not believe in God because they believe in science. While this is another book altogether, I would be remiss if I did not mention the correlation between passionless healthcare providers, the tendency for providers to be scientists, and the belief in science versus faith when it comes to the universe and our existence/creation. Too many healthcare professionals lack faith, and thus they lack a passion and purpose for what they are doing.

I myself have to be honest and tell you that I almost fell into these statistics because I allowed the profession to tear me down mentally, physically, and emotionally. I found myself "working" in my dream career that I didn't choose, but instead chose me. I was making decent money and was comfortable. However, on the inside, I was unhappy, miserable, and depressed! I would often find myself questioning God, and if I can be honest with you, I was a little mad and confused as to why God was allowing me to suffer this way. My talks with Him went something like this: *"God, so did you really call me to healthcare to work 12-hour shifts with six patients, of which three are total care and the other three need IV pushes every two hours? To add insult to injury, these six families keep coming to my station every other hour asking new questions, and on top of that, my feet feel like rocks! Really, God? I know this is what I am called to do, but I don't like it and I want to quit!"* I began to feel burnt out, broken, busted and disgusted because I did not have a purpose to my career choices. Now don't get me wrong, I took very good care of my patients, made a difference in their lives and learned so much, but I still felt like (and asked the Lord), *"OK, so this is it? Is this all you called me to do, God?"*

For me, these feelings of purposelessness, uselessness and brokenness were a result of being unintentional. I felt like this for about five more years as I migrated to various areas of nursing, hoping that I would find the "job" that would fill the void that I was feeling. I wasn't being purposeful at all, and I desperately wanted to be in health-care on purpose. On my desperate search for the position that would make me feel complete, I found myself running in circles. None of these positions made me feel like I was living life on purpose. Honestly, the feelings of uselessness, misery and unhappiness grew stronger and stronger...

Finally, I crashed and burned, and I gave up! I gave up because I realized that what I was doing just was not working. I was so hurt, broken and unfulfilled. Eventually, my thinking became: *Nicole, just be happy that you have a job. This is all that it will ever be, so you might as well stop complaining, be satisfied, and wait on your direct deposit every two weeks.* Although reality told me to just be satisfied with where I was, there was something that kept tugging at me. I was dissatisfied. I was disgusted. There was something tugging at me (*There had to be more to my career*); it just wouldn't leave me alone. And that is when things changed. I need you to get something very important here. Nothing will change in your life or about your career as long as you can still tolerate it. When you get to the point where your current circumstances become intolerable, you will be forced to take the step to change them.

I have always been a spiritual person, but I still managed to get lost because I was not plugged into the outlet tightly. I wavered because I was not consistent and my faith was lackluster. Eventually, I discovered that if I wanted to be purpose-filled (meaning filled with purpose day in and out) I had to be awakened to my purpose in healthcare. I decided to secure my plug firmly into the socket, and I went back to the one constant that had been in my life all along — which was the word of God. As soon as I found my way back to God's word, I was reintroduced to a scripture that opened my eyes and changed my thinking:

*"The purposes of a person's heart are deep waters,
but one who has insight draws them out."*
Proverbs 20:5 (NIV)

Some translations of that verse read, "The plans of a person's heart…" To put this into perspective, I realized that I was born with a divine purpose (or plan from God) as a healthcare professional and either I was going to discover it or I was going to miss it!

Refuse to miss it

At that moment I knew if I wanted to experience a life of purpose and truly know I was making a difference in this profession, I had to do something that I had never done before — do the self-work to discover why God called me to healthcare in the first place. Why did the Lord *choose* me to be a nurse? Why was this calling placed on my life? In order to gain a true understanding of what God had in mind when He created me and my purpose, I had to go deep into places that I had never been and ask questions that I was not quite ready to know the answers to. I had to ask questions that would force me to face some of my biggest fears and revisit some places from the past. Whether I knew it or not back then, there were things that happened in my life even long before I was in healthcare that aligned with where God wanted me to end up. Those places had been designed to conceive my purpose. Think back on your own life. When did you first begin to feel the desire to "help people?" What made you want to nurture others or learn the ins and outs of the human body? What experiences from your past helped you get to where you are today? What are the common threads and the common skills that you have used in each place or position?

I asked myself a series of questions. Here they are along with my answers. This process was life changing for me:

1. Why do I *need to* know my purpose as a healthcare professional?

I had to get fed up with my current circumstances, in order to find the courage to change them.

2. When I transition to the other side, what type of healthcare provider do I want to be remembered as?

I realized that I wanted to be remembered as a community servant that educated vulnerable communities on how to live healthier lives. I wanted to be known as the nurse who was an innovator and pushed passed all limits, a human being that lived her life authentically and on purpose.

3. What am I passionate about as a healthcare professional?

I am passionate about educating and empowering others to be the best versions of themselves that they can be.

4. What am I naturally good at?

I am great at educating.

5. What brought me joy as a child?

I enjoyed talking and being with others.

6. What things am I doing as a healthcare professional and in my personal life that do not bring me joy and fulfillment?

I realized that I was not being innovative and educating others like I wanted to, without restriction, and that caused me great misery.

7. When it is all said and done, what matters the most to me as a human being and as a healthcare professional, and am I on track with this right now?

What matters the most to me is that I lived the life that God has for me and not the one man has for me. I wasn't on track with that then, but I am on track with God's purpose for me now.

These are just a few of the many questions (and answers) that I asked myself to discover my divine purpose as a healthcare provider. I tried to avoid answering certain questions because, on one hand, they forced me to face fears that I had, acknowledge personal habits or faults that I needed to change, and identify responsibilities or skills that I really wasn't good at. On the other hand, facing the answers to these questions provided me a breath of fresh air. Facing the reality that I was totally unhappy being a floor nurse [this is not a slight to floor nursing. At one point, I, in fact, loved it but knew it wasn't where I was supposed to be forever] made me realize what I loved and what I disliked about my career. Answering the question "What am I passionate about as a healthcare professional?" made me face the facts that I am designed to be an innovator, educator and thought leader. The nursing roles that I had in the past were simply my transportation to my destiny. I could not be a traditional floor nurse that worked 12-hour shifts forever. Nor was I designed to be a home health nurse that worked in the field all day. I couldn't have the normal limitations with time and place of assignments. I realized that I loved creating initiatives and finding ways to highlight people who were doing amazing work. I couldn't think of a way to merge all of the things that I loved into one position, and so I realized that I was designed to be an entrepreneur and a nurse — a nursepreneur. I was finally being honest about some things that I was unhappy with and I now had the courage to dig them up. These questions and this process of facing myself, my thoughts and my pains led to discovering MY purpose as a healthcare professional. These questions connected my personal being to my professional being, and the answers married both sides of me so that I could finally conceive my baby — my purpose as a healthcare professional.

Oftentimes we come into healthcare with the best intentions. We show up every day, happy, and on time. We give our all to those we care for. We give our all to our employers or employees. We lose sleep over tough cases. We miss meals, and we lose ourselves in the midst of all that we do. Then gradually over time, we look up and realize that while we were so busy taking care of everyone else and making everyone else happy, we became totally unfulfilled. After that, we fall into the trap of making it all about the Benjamins or going through the motions of going to work because this is what we have to do in order to make a living. We settle and we fall into the trap of despising the very profession that we chose. Some of us work in a certain aspect of healthcare because we have too much pride to admit to our family and friends that we are not fulfilled, *and yes,* we are unhappy, despite going to school and spending dozens of thousands of dollars on a degree. We don't want to be viewed as failures or quitters, so we continue to merely show up every day. We settle for living a life without purpose.

These are all unfortunate commonalities of many healthcare professionals. But why do they have to be? Why are we spending thousands of dollars to receive professional degrees or to attend colleges and universities if we don't feel the desire to do so? Why are we placing our lives on hold for four-plus years while we attend school, take courses and dedicate ourselves to learning and passing mandated standardized tests? Why are we persistent and why do we give our all to enter a field that we have little passion for? Why do we feel like our titles and salaries define us? Why are we doing all of this without knowing the purpose behind it? I wanted to know the answers, so I found statistical data on why healthcare professionals become unfulfilled, thus contributing to them losing sight of their purpose and leaving the industry.

The top reason why healthcare professionals are not in health on purpose is because of the long hours that most of us are required to work. I know that all of my nurses can relate to this one as most of us at some point in time have worked 12-hour shifts, with rotating weekends and little to no breaks. Our demanding schedules cause debilitating health issues and force us to miss out on precious family time. We lose ourselves because we fail to take care of ourselves.

The second reason why professionals are not in health on purpose is because they feel obligated to perform tasks that are not appropriate for the level they are at. For example, a floor nurse may be irritated if she has to complete standardized paperwork such as a patient's basic health information like primary care physician, allergies, etc. that should have been completed prior to the patient entering her unit. No matter your role as a healthcare professional, you can probably relate to this example and recall a time when you had to do a job that was below your pay grade. We are often too qualified to be doing many of the basic-level tasks that we must do. Always having to do multiple jobs or tasks that are considered to be "entry level" will begin to take a toll on anyone.

The third reason why professionals are not in health on purpose is because they work in hostile environments. You may be wondering how can healthcare be hostile. Perhaps if you work in the emergency room or a mental health ward or facility, you may be silently screaming YESSS because you can relate all too well to "hostile healthcare environments." As healthcare professionals, we often go into situations blindly, not knowing *important* conditions that our patients are facing. Family dynamics is a big one. For instance, there may be a wife who is fleeing an abusive spouse. OK, so what happens when that intrusive, rude and hostile husband learns that his wife has been admitted into your facility and shows up while you are the attending healthcare professional? Now you are caught in the middle of a domestic dispute, and you have to get involved by either asking the spouse to leave or by contacting the security department or police.

Your main priority is to maintain the safety of everyone in your facility and to prevent this situation from becoming violent. You have just traded in your scrubs for an invisible badge, but no gun. Of course, you are a bit nervous because *you know that if it becomes violent,* you will be caught in the middle of a fight or worse — crossfire. In urban communities, this risk of violence in an emergency room is not off base.

There are also hostile work environments caused by co-worker issues. Healthcare professionals are required to work as teams, often as one unit, and so despite any hostility due to personal issues, we must still keep the team intact. This can easily turn into workplace bullying and disrespect. Who wants to work in these situations and who wouldn't feel discouraged and question their purpose as a healthcare professional under either of these circumstances?

The fourth reason people are not in health on purpose is due to pay. I am sure I don't have to tell you much about this one, as you are fully aware that the money you thought you would make or you feel that you deserve (compared to how much you actually earn) is not exactly what you are bringing in every two weeks. Despite what many believe, most healthcare professionals do not make a huge income when compared to therequirements and obligations that are placed upon them. According to the U.S. Bureau of Labor Statistics, the average salary of a seasoned nurse is $66,000. This is a nurse who has at least five to seven years of service. The U.S. Bureau of Labor Statistics also indicates that the average salary of a physician is $187,000. Now before you say, "Oh that is a lot of money..." Remember, this is for a physician that has been practicing for a minimum of ten years, and who practices in highly specialized fields. The average income for a seasoned physical therapist is $82,000, with the key word being "seasoned" that means this is after five to seven years of experience. This average salary also depends on location, place of employment and experience. The perceived income level for healthcare professionals and what many of us feel they should be earning do not measure up to increasing work demands, long hours, high risk of compromised safety, and many other elements that contribute to feelings of whether it's all even worth it. No matter how noble a profession this may be or what originally attracted a person to the healthcare industry, income is always tied to feelings of worthiness. If income requirements are not filled, health-care professionals lose sight of their role and many leave the profession.

The fifth reason that people are not in health on purpose is due to poor management. Let's face it, how we perform, how much effort we put in, how devoted we are, and how much we are willing to take is often tied to the type of leadership we are under. Great leaders inspire employees to be great. But on the other hand, if I as an employee have a leader who does not invest in me or my professional development, who does not care about my responsibilities, fails to help me learn, fails to be accessible, who is not credible or knows his/her job, why would I be motivated to excel? It would become obvious to me very early on that this manager does not care about me, and he/she simply wants me to show up and get the job done. The picture I just painted was based on my own personal experiences, and these experiences had a huge role in my feelings of non-fulfillment as a nurse. I often hear this same scenario described to me by my colleagues day in and out. For some reason, the American healthcare industry has produced an overwhelming amount of purpose-less leaders, who are inspiring a generation of purpose-less professionals, and causing the rate of professionals in healthcare to diminish rapidly. We must find a way to get back to inspiring and producing healthcare professionals who are in health, on purpose.

One important factor causing the decline of purpose-filled healthcare professionals that was omitted from the research is that many healthcare professionals are not intentional in how they choose their careers, how they navigate in their careers and choose their roles. Too many people lose sight of what they want and where they belong, and they have failed to ask the million-dollar-question, "God, why did you call me to healthcare?" Once you know the "why" and you discover your purpose, then you will become intentional. At that point, none of the risks we listed above will affect you because you will be focused on your personal purpose. You will not feel unfulfilled because you will know your "why." Despite all that you will endure as a healthcare professional, you will know that it is for a greater purpose, and that purpose is bigger than you and any temporary circumstance that may affect you at work. Focusing on the reasons why we were "called" is the single most effective way to revive our industry with profession-als who are in health, on purpose.

Remember those questions I referenced earlier that I had to ask myself? Now it's your turn to ask yourself those same questions.

Why do I *need to* know my purpose as a healthcare professional?

_____

_____

_____

_____

_____

_____

_____

_____

_____

When I transition to the other side, what type of healthcare provider do I want to be remembered as?

_____

_____

_____

_____

_____

_____

_____

_____

What am I passionate about as a healthcare professional? Why am I passionate about this?

_____

_____

_____

_____

_____

_____

_____

_____

_____

_____

What brought me joy as a child? Why did this bring me so much joy?

_____

_____

_____

_____

_____

_____

_____

What things am I doing as a healthcare professional and in my personal life that do not bring me joy and fulfillment?

_____

_____

_____

_____

_____

_____

_____

_____

Why do I continue to do things despite them not bringing me joy?

_____

_____

_____

_____

_____

_____

_____

_____

_____

_____

When it is all said and done, what matters the most to me as a human being and as a healthcare professional, and am I on track with this right now?

_____

_____

_____

_____

_____

_____

_____

_____

_____

_____

_____

_____

Chapter 4:
Regaining Control of Your Purpose

It does not matter what you lost; what matters is what you have left because God is going to use what you have left to bring you out of your dark valley and use you for His glory. These are the words that my "mentor," Bishop T.D. Jakes spoke to me one day as I was listening to his sermon. At the time I was in a place where I had hit rock bottom. I was totally depleted of the will power to continue working as a nurse. I wanted OUT. I was tired of being depressed. I was tired of crying. My mental state had begun to take a physical toll on my body. Bishop Jakes' words literally shook something up in me and let me know, *"Nicole, you are not going down without a fight!"* I knew at that point that I was going to stand flat footed, planted in the word of God, and I would take back what the enemy had stolen from me. At the time that included my purpose as a healthcare professional. I realized in that moment that I didn't choose healthcare, God chose healthcare for me. Listening to those words made me realize that I would win this fight and that I had a purpose. I couldn't quit just because I had lost control and sight of what God had predestined for my life.

Losing sight of why you do what you do is frustrating, hurtful and often leads to depression. Although I have never been an attorney, an architect or a mechanic, I can imagine that for us healthcare professionals it is even more frustrating than in other professions when we lose sight of our purpose because we realize that we have the lives of others in our hands. I myself can recall times in which I would be in the middle of taking care of a patient who was suffering from a life-threatening disease. Although I still took really good care of this patient, there was a disconnect. I felt like I was just going through the motions and was not fully invested in being a purposeful nurse. I wasn't being intentional about connecting with my patients and their families in more than just a physical way. As healthcare professionals, this feeling "out of it" is one of the worst emotions we can feel. It's almost like we are sleepwalking through our careers — while fires and storms are brewing around us.

When there is a total disconnect from your "why" or when you have lost sight of your purpose, the first thing you must do is regain control. I wish I could tell you that it will be an easy overnight process, and that it will feel good, that it will be smooth sailing… oh, how I wish I could tell you that, but I am going to be completely honest with you. Regaining a handle of what has you in this career is not an overnight process. In fact, it will not feel good, and it will be as rough as the waters of a stormy sea at times. It will be uncomfortable and frustrating, but it will be worth it. The process of finding you — reconnecting with your true purpose as a healthcare professional — has many long-term benefits. So, if you have realized that you too have been sleepwalking through your career, maybe you've begun to feel disgusted, bored, unsure or unfulfilled, it is time to roll up your sleeves and begin the process of regaining control of why God has called you to this work. Let's get into some things that you can start doing right now that will put you well on your way to regaining your purpose (and vision) as a healthcare professional.

1. Make the choice. Before we can begin to correct anything in life, we have to make a personal choice that *"I am committed to doing the work to become the change that I want to see."* This may sound simple, but it's the necessary first step in creating change and living in health on purpose. We all have choices to make each day, and choices to make when it comes to our lives. If we choose wisely, we'll end up with promising results. To the contrary, when our choices reflect poor decision-making, laziness or being misinformed, our results tend to be just as dismal. So you have to make a choice to begin the journey of discovering your purpose. It's easy to simply stay in the same space. It is easy to stay secure in your current position and dissatisfied, yet comfortable with your salary, benefits, and work environment. It is even easy to complain and become a part of the peanut gallery of disgruntled staff who are all unfulfilled in their positions. Those things are easy, but it will be much more difficult to make a choice — to decide to change and stick with that decision. Making a choice to change your life is not always easy. So what will you do? If you are committed to this first step, you can move on to the next.

2. Change your mindset. This is probably one of the most challenging steps in regaining our purpose as healthcare professionals because we become accustomed to how we operate and our own ways of thinking and doing things. But change can never occur in the current state of your mind because the current state is what has you in the present state of mind that you are in. It's impossible to take old thinking and ways of doing things into a future place of destiny. Changing your mindset will require you to adopt several new habits. You will need to replace your old data that you've been working with all these years with new data. You'll need to "renew your mind," as the Bible says, and that begins with the word of God. So I highly recommend getting in the word. You also have to admit to yourself that you need a change of mind. Identify some of the barriers that have limited your thinking or limited your growth.

Perhaps you have had barriers in your career because you subscribed to someone else's way of thinking. Maybe while you were in school, you only learned of a few ways that someone in your field can operate or make a living and so you figured that you had to do things like this too. Maybe people told you that you would not be successful doing things the way you wanted to do them, and so you gave up on certain dreams. What are the mental barriers that you have subscribed to or that have attached themselves to you by way of environment or others? What type of thinking has led you to the place that you are in now? It's important to recognize this. Identifying the mental barriers that you've subscribed to will help you pinpoint the exact thinking that is working contrary to what you want to achieve. Once you identify the thoughts that are toxic to your purpose, you can begin to speak against those thoughts.

3. Change your language. Life and death lie in the power of the tongue! (Proverbs 18:21) You are what you speak and you become what you say. So start declaring that you are purposeful as a healthcare professional, that you are intentional, that everything you are going through is working for your good, that you are fearless, that you are courageous, that you are more than a conqueror, that you are successful, that everything that you were once seeking is now seeking you. These are just a few of the declarations that you should be speaking over your life and career daily. The Bible says that if you seek, you shall find. So now that you are actively seeking to live in health on purpose, you shall confidently speak all of the previous declarations with no problems or hesitations. In the previous step, we talked about changing your mindset. What you speak is just as important as what you think. You should be making confessions of faith. In the Amplified version of Mark 4:24, Jesus teaches us this: *"Pay attention to what you hear. By your own standard of measurement [that is, to the extent that you study spiritual truth and apply godly wisdom] it will be measured to you [and you will be given even greater ability to respond] — and more will be given to you besides."*

Here is my daily affirmation that I read daily, multiple times a day to remind myself of who God says I am versus what Man says I am.

Daily Affirmations
I will hear the voice of the Holy spirit within me.
I will lead and not follow.
I will create and not destroy.
I set new standards.
I defy the odds.
I am a leader.
I am the head and not the tail.
I am above and not beneath.
I am a lender and not a borrower.
I am loved by God.
I am chosen by God.
I am protected by God.
No weapon formed against me shall prosper.

And every tongue that rises up against me in judgment
shall be condemned.
Everything I touch turns to gold.
Everything I'm seeking is now seeking me.
It's my season.
It's my turn.
I am humble.
I am happy.
I am wealthy.
I am strong.
I am a champion.
I will never be broke another day in my life.
I am created for greatness.
I am in health on purpose.
AND SO IT IS.

4. Explore your options. It is not enough to simply change your thoughts, change your speech and to make a decision. The next step in your process of living in health on purpose is to explore your options. Realize that you have no ceiling. So explore. Identify others in your area of healthcare or even your place of employment who seem to be living on purpose. Don't limit yourself to those you can physically see and touch either. Inspiration and new revelations of your own possibilities can come from various places. In college, many students are taught to request informational interviews with people who are in their fields. I believe this can be just as beneficial to experienced healthcare professionals who are seeking purpose. Request meetings or conversations with those whom you admire and people who are walking and thriving in their purpose. Ask them questions about their day-to-day lives, what does it take to do what they do day in and out? Find out the limitations they face, any barriers that they've experienced, etc. Create a short list of five people whom you can reach out to, and begin to make connections. Begin to research other resources, websites, blogs, coaches, and others from which you can glean inspiration and wisdom.

5. Be courageous. Many people feel that being fearless means to have no fear at all when actually being fearless means being courageous enough to overcome the fear. We are all humans and fleshly people so fear and doubt will creep in. That's the enemy's job. However, you must be courageous and hold your head up high and push through. It takes courage to overcome fear. Fear is a natural feeling whenever you are starting something new. When you shake things up, there is a natural fear of the unknown and that is perfectly alright. However, don't allow this *temporary* fear to grip you. Keep pressing forward in your journey. Start with small steps (identified in steps 1-4) and then begin to make tangible changes.

6. Get to know God for yourself. You can only get to know God through His word. *In the beginning was the Word, and the Word was with God, and the Word was God.* (John 1:1) Because God and His word are one, you must get to know the word of God for yourself in order to have a true relationship with God. This will develop your faith in God and also faith in your journey and yourself. Faith comes by hearing and hearing by the word of God. (Romans 10:17) So begin to add a daily regimen of the word in your life. As you read the word and allow it to saturate your spirit, God's voice will become clear to you. Promises from God will begin to resonate with you, and you'll grow more confident in His promises. Living in health on purpose isn't a manufactured state of being. It is very much so a spiritual process. You must partner with God in your journey to purpose. He will reveal your purpose once He knows you are ready and He can trust you with it. Remember that our lives are not our own. We were all put here to accomplish a specific purpose for God. He wants you to be in health on purpose, just as much as you want to be. He has something to accomplish through you, and so you must become one with Him, and seek Him with all of your heart.

7. Make your passion your priority. In the introduction, I talked about passion. Your purpose should be your passion. So right now, even before it all makes sense to you, begin to follow your passion. You will need to go through some of the questions that I shared with you about my own process of discovery (refer to Chapter 3). Make lists of what you love to do. What gives you great joy, and also what problems irritate you the most. Irritation in this sense is a good thing. It means that you are so moved about an issue that you are compelled to change it or address it. You cannot ignore an irritation. Just think when your scalp or nose itches, or when you have an irritating ache or pain — you can't just ignore those irritations. You have to address them and confront them. You have to get to the root of the itch, the pain or the ache. No one is going to just sit around and be irritated without confronting that irritation. You must handle it. Our purpose is the same way. For me, one of the areas that irritated me was that so many healthcare professionals were not living in health on purpose. I couldn't sit around and watch my peers suffer without addressing it and contributing to a solution. That's what a passion and a purpose will feel like to you. If there is something that you simply cannot ignore, you have to develop a solution or contribute to a better way — this is most likely a piece of your purpose puzzle. Identify these areas. And make your response to them a priority.

Remember, however, that just because you are good at something (or have been doing it for a long time), it doesn't mean that it is your purpose. A major part of regaining control of your purpose is identifying those things that you enjoy doing, those things that you are good at doing and those things that you can't imagine NOT doing.

Because you are great at something, it does not mean you are destined to stay there. Sometimes our talents are simply tools God gives us to accomplish our purpose versus the exact purpose He has for us.

We've addressed a lot in this chapter, and while it may be overwhelming at first, remember to start small. Just as you would learn various lessons all semester to prepare for your final exam, taking small steps toward your purpose will prepare you to actually walk in the manifestation of that promise God has for you. Don't try to go in head first and change things up immediately.

Remember you are on God's time. Allow yourself to go through the mental, emotional and spiritual process of self-discovery and purpose discovery. As you go through this process, you will begin to remove things that do not fit into that purpose puzzle, and soon you will have regained controlled of God's ultimate plan and purpose for your career.

Lastly, never forget the words of Bishop T.D. Jakes: "It doesn't matter what you lost; what matters is what you have left, because God is going to use what you have left to bring you out, and use you for His glory."

Remember changing your language is definitely one of the most critical changes you can make today to begin regaining your purpose. I shared my personal affirmations earlier in this chapter, and below I want you to create your own. Changing your language — renewing your purpose, starts today!

My Daily Affirmations
(List in Present Tense)

_____

_____

_____

_____

_____

_____

_____

_____

_____

_____

_____

_____

_____

_____

_____

_____

_____

_____

_____

_____

_____

_____

_____

Take your daily affirmations to the next level, and post them everywhere you go throughout the day (i.e. your bathroom, your car, your closet, on the refrigerator, etc.) and read these affirmations every time you see them until they are embedded into your subconscious mind. There is a template at the end of the book that will allow you to duplicate the above.

In Health, On Purpose!

Chapter 5:
From Purpose to Impact

Do the names Florence Nightingale, Clara Barton, Lillian Holland Harvey or Lillian Wald ring a bell? Now I know for sure all of my nurse colleagues have heard of these names because they have been embedded in us from the time we stepped foot on the nursing school's grounds. Nevertheless, if you have never heard of these names, let me help you out. Each of these individuals has been coined as pioneers in the nursing profession. These women made their own impact on the world of nursing and healthcare. For example, Florence Nightingale worked tirelessly to improve sanitation and hospital conditions, and to ensure that nurses were adequately trained. She leveraged her relationships with government officials, businessmen, and the military, and created a Campaign for Action to strengthen the nursing profession. Then there is Clara Barton, who was the lead organizer in the formation of the American Red Cross in the late 1800s. The United States initially rejected the Red Cross because the government did not feel this new organization was necessary. We see how untrue that was and how a single health professional has had an impact on our country's relief efforts. Today, whenever there is a major disaster or a humanitarian emergency we call on the American Red Cross. Then there is Lillian Holland Harvey, a nurse leader and an educator, who created the first Bachelor of Science degree nursing program at Tuskegee University. She was passionate about educating and leading others to greatness, and her impact has led to equal educational opportunities for nurses all over the world. And last but not least, there is Lillian Wald, who was born into wealth and used her economic and social status to serve vulnerable communities through the formation of the Henry Street Settlement, a community resources center that addresses healthcare disparities in New York City. The Henry Street Settlement changed the way healthcare was delivered in a community approach.

As you can see, these women — all pioneers in nursing coming from various walks of life — each brought something totally different to the healthcare profession. The one similarity that they each had in common was purposeful IMPACT. They utilized their gifts, talents, resources and passions to fulfill their God-ordained purpose in the healthcare profession. If you are a healthcare professional, no matter what you are doing right now, these women should inspire you to see that more is possible. In fact, more is destined when you are in health, on purpose.

If I could only share one piece of advice, a jewel of wisdom, with you, it would be: "Your purpose is in you but not for you." I am going to get really straightforward here: If you keep your purpose to yourself, you are being downright SELFISH. It is selfish because God placed each of us here, no matter our past, for a specific reason and one reason only — and that is to be a part of HIS plan to change the earth. If you fail to seek and discover your purpose and to use your purpose to impact change, you will never be totally happy and successful. Successful people based on the Lord's standards (not the world's) are people who are living in God's purpose for their lives. There is something that you AND ONLY YOU can bring to the earth in your role as a healthcare professional. Regardless of how many other people do what you do, no one else can do it like you can do it. If you refuse to share your purpose with the world, you are being self-centered and downright disrespectful toward God. Let's put this into perspective. I'm not sure if you can relate to this analogy, but let's just imagine for a moment that you are a mother or father. You give birth to a child, you invest all of your resources into that child, regardless of the heartaches, pain and trouble that they may put you through, you stick it out with them. The reason that you do this is because you know through all of it, your child is a diamond and a lot has been invested in them. You have faith that one day all that you have poured in throughout the years will come out in the form of your child's specific work or purpose on earth.

To the contrary, despite all of your investments of time and resources, your child may reject everything you have poured into them, and decide to take a totally wrong turn in life. They decide to then take everything you've invested — the good morals, principles, values and even the prayers —and use those things for their own personal agenda. Their agenda does not involve helping anyone but themselves. They refuse to even help you, after all that you have done for them! The first thing you would wonder as a parent, is *How did this child become so selfish?* You would probably feel that your child is being outright disrespectful. Now imagine how your Father in Heaven would feel with you, His child whom He loves and adores, if you ignore the one reason why He gave you life. Think of it this way. Instead of breathing life into you, God could have selected anyone else to give life to and give your purpose to. But instead, He selected you and filled you up with everything that will be necessary for you to accomplish that which you were created for.

Earlier, I stated that your purpose is in you, but not for you. Your purpose is here to serve others and make an impact in some manner. And I know many people think to themselves, *how can little ole me make a huge impact?* Honestly, that is not for you to worry about because God will take care of all of that. Your job is to submit to Him and to be obedient. Once that happens, He will make provisions and ensure that the impact that He wants your life to have will be accomplished. He will begin to put His divine plan for you into action by aligning you with the right people, resources, and tools on purpose. Sometimes we get very caught up in the HOW rather than focusing on the WHO.

Take me, for an example. I have had a passion for education and leadership for over 15 years. I would complete trainings, in-services, and leadership courses while keeping the knowledge that I learned all to myself. I would take necessary steps to develop myself as a leader but would be afraid to actually lead when the opportunities would present themselves because I was so worried about "how" I would lead others. I was being selfish, self-centered and disrespectful by not using the education and leadership knowledge that I had obtained. I was keeping all of this greatness within me rather than sharing it. I was operating in fear. I worried for no reason because God had already predestined me with a specific purpose. He had already decided to use me as a vessel. He wanted me to bless others with my knowledge and support others with the impeccable leadership skills that He had blessed me with.

What if Steve Jobs kept his vision to develop

innovative technology to himself? What if he was too scared, worried, busy or selfish to move forward on his first idea to develop a product called the Apple I Board? What if he and two of his close friends had never formed Apple, Inc. in 1976, and failed to follow their passion of developing computers? What if Steve Jobs and his Apple co-founders doubted their resources and deemed the garage where they began building computers as insufficient? If even one of these "what ifs" were true, we would not benefit from the life-changing impact on communications, technology, and life as we know it — nor would we have Apple Inc., the iPhone, iPad, Apple Watch and more. Thank God that Steve Jobs was obedient to his purpose. The world with no Apple, MacBooks, iPads or iPhones would be a completely different world. How selfish would it have been for Steve Jobs to withhold his gifts, talents, and ideas from the world?

Do you see where I am going with this? Each of these examples is of real people who lived on purpose and made a tremendous impact in the world. What's even better about all of these individuals, is that none of them had to do anything extravagant to make an impact. They simply pursued their purpose and followed their passions.

Now, what about you? For a moment can you imagine the way you will use your purpose to make an impact? When nurses, nurse practitioners, therapists and allied healthcare professionals in the future discover your life and Google your name, what will Google tell them about you? Will your name even come up in the search results? More importantly, what will those who will be blessed with your impact in our present day say about you? You have a significant contribution to make in the healthcare profession. What will that contribution be?

Below begin to visualize the impact you will make:

I will use my purpose in healthcare to make an impact on my community or family through:

_____

_____

My purpose will make an impact on the following specific groups of people or parts of society:

_____

_____

Through my purpose in healthcare, I can partner with others in the following industries to make an even bigger impact:

_____

_____

I am going to start small first. I will begin making my long-term impact through the following program/project:

_____

_____

I cannot do this on my own, so I am going to seek the help of (list 3-5 people):

_____

_____

If you know the answer to these questions and you are actively working on making an impact great, and if you do not know the answers to these questions but know that you have something that you and only you can leave with the healthcare industry, then that is great too. Either way, you realize that you have something in you, and you are about to use your purpose to make an impact. So let's get to it and move from purpose to impact.

Here are five non-negotiables that will help you move from purpose to impact:

Be unapologetically and authentically YOU. OK, so I am here to tell you from firsthand experience that not everyone will understand why you are doing what you are doing. Some will think that it is the silliest and craziest thing that they have ever heard of, and yes that will include those close to you as well as strangers. But it is OK because the thing about your purpose is that it is yours, and it was given to you and not to anyone else. It is not their job to understand why you are doing what you are doing, but it is your responsibility to fulfill your God-ordained purpose as a healthcare professional. Do not try to convince people why you are going back to school when they feel you have enough degrees, or why you are opening a business when your credentials and respective licensing board says your role in healthcare is to operate in a particular scope, or why you are going to attend workshops and seminars about becoming a public speaker or influencer, when they feel that you serve better behind the scenes. Now by all means, please be open to effective and constructive criticism from reliable sources because it will help you to become a better you on your journey of purpose to impact, but don't get caught up into those who criticize what you are doing because of their limited views.

Keep your emotions in check. The number one reason that many people do not pursue their purpose, which can be impactful, is because they get all into their feelings. Emotions will make you do things that you should not do, such

61

as allow people into your circle who are not suppose to be with you on your journey from purpose to impact because you like the way they make you feel. These people will influence you to make decisions that are emotionally based versus Holy-spirit based. This can have a negative impact on your purpose as a healthcare professional and prevent you from receiving wisdom from God.

Be in tune with your strengths and weaknesses. The most successful people have areas where they dominate and those that they do not. For the weaker areas, successful people seek outside assistance. No person who has achieved any type of success did so because they could dominate in every area. Instead, they were smart enough to hire the right people. The point is you have to know you and know how to build off of your strengths and weaknesses. Without this, you will not be able to turn your purpose to impact.

Build a killer team. I don't how many people I meet who ask me, "Nicole, how do you manage being a wife, mother, mentor, business woman, nurse, and friend?" My answer is my team! There is not a way that I can do all these things effectively and at a level of excellence without having a killer team. Seek those people to join your team who can assist you in your areas where you are weak, who are smarter than you, who totally identify and buy into your vision. I can't tell you how many people have a team and still don't ever get to a point where they can make an impact. Trust me I have experienced this myself when I had a "team" of people who did not have the same principles, vision, or work ethic as me, and I got nowhere, literally. I never moved from purpose to impact until I developed a killer team that was "ride or die" for me.

Go big or go home. The way I see it, the way my God works — He who is the Jehovah-Nissi (The Lord my banner), Jehovah-Jireh (The Lord my provider), Jehovah-Eli (The Lord my God), Jehovah-Shalom (The Lord of peace), and Jehovah-'Izoa Hakaboth (The Lord strong and mighty) — I can't think small. Here is what I mean by that: I need my dreams, goals, and aspirations to be so big that everyone who sees the fulfillment of them knows that it was nobody but God who could have done it because it was outside of my human capabilities to do something of that magnitude. God gets the glory and not I. So, go BIG!

In Health, On Purpose!

Chapter 6:

Leaving Your Legacy

··

There will come a day when you will no longer be on earth. Have you imagined that day? What will be said during your eulogy, and how will people remember you? What do you want your family, friends or colleagues to say about you when they have three minutes to describe your life and the impact you had on theirs? I know these are uncomfortable conversations to have, but these are the exact questions you should be asking yourself as a nurse, nurse practitioner, therapist or allied health professional. Will you be remembered by a legacy or will people just know your title? While there is nothing wrong with having a title(s), remember the nurses that we discussed in Chapter 5 who made a significant impact on society — despite a title. The thing that set them apart was not only their impact while they were here, but the legacy they left behind. Think beyond your title now to create your legacy.

I answered the questions above for myself, and to think about the day that I will die was uncomfortable and difficult. I knew it was necessary if I wanted my ordained purpose as a nurse to leave an impact and a legacy. I knew that I wanted the nurses who come after me to remember me for my legacy, the way we remember Florence Nightingale, Clara Barton, Lillian Holland Harvey and Lillian Wald. I wrote out my "Legacy Statement." This is the general idea that I want people to remember or say about me when I am gone. It goes like this:

Nicole had a passion for learning the latest successful evidence-based healing practices to help heal the sick. She aimed to invest the knowledge she learned in others so that they too could become well-educated. Through her passion she boldly, courageously and un-apologetically walked in her purpose as a nurse providing education, mentoring and leading fellow healthcare professionals to greatness. Nicole was a true servant who never made her career about her, but allowed God to show through her.

Merriam-Webster Dictionary describes *legacy* as "something transmitted by or received from an ancestor or predecessor or from the past." For a moment, think about this, *What will I transmit to the future? What will the future receive from me?* Those questions are powerful. From Clara Barton, we received healing and a relief resource, and from Florence Nightingale, we received healing and education. For most people in healthcare, our legacy will come down to what we give, how we serve and who we serve. Will you provide education, healing, ideas, resources, community… or will you simply show up, get paid and go home?

Most of the nurses that I have mentioned in this book have been notable examples of individuals who have been *In Health, On Purpose!* However, I do not want you to think for one moment that your impact has to end up on Wikipedia or in textbooks for you to have a legacy. The two things that you can do today to ensure your legacy for tomorrow is to decide to live and work in purpose and to begin making an impact on the people and communities who are closest to you. It will be a tremendous mistake if you decide after reading this book to travel to some far-off land to begin providing healthcare services, without ever addressing the needs and concerns of the people God has placed in your life where you are today. You do not have to search far to make a difference. There will be someone near you or those who God will send to you whom you can serve immediately. Your legacy will be established by the small difference you make in the lives of everyday individuals.

In the previous chapter, you visualized the type of impact you want to make. Your legacy will come by actually pursuing what you've visualized — your purpose — and serving those who God has assigned to your life. It will not be forced. It will not be a strain, and it will not be a matter of "trying." You will simply become intentional, from this day forward, about waking up every morning with the intent to live in health on purpose. As a matter of fact, you should be excited each morning to wake up, and begin living out the purpose God has designed for you. Pray to Him throughout the day *every day* that He constantly guides you and provides you with opportunities to discover and serve Him in your purpose. Your legacy will be solidified once you make each day about serving God on purpose, and that will mean that you serve His people. This will not be easy. You will be inconvenienced. You will be irritated some days. But during those moments of irritations, be very aware of whether God is calling you to do more — address your concerns and the concerns of others — always ask yourself how does your experience and talents fit with this current situation? Begin looking for ways to make a difference in the roles that you have. It's just like being a physician — a physician will seek and search for the illness within the patient and the way they can help solve that problem and remedy their patients' pains. Those people who are assigned to your life are your patients. You have a cure or a remedy to what they are facing, and now you simply have to prescribe the correct medicine to treat their situation.

God has equipped you with everything that you need to accomplish the purpose that He has designed you for. He has already done everything that He will ever do, and the Bible tells us that He has already blessed you with what you need — because you are His child (Ephesians 1:3). Because you are his child, He will give you the desires of your heart that align with His will and the purpose that He has for your life, which includes your professional career as a healthcare provider. When people who are close to me look at my big dreams with a side eye, I say, "I am the child of the King, so everything has to make room for me." Once I allowed God to speak to me through the Holy Spirit on what He wants for my life, no matter how big or small, I developed that mentality. So it is time for you to stop asking for permission, and instead serve notice, because you are enough!

I grew up in a vulnerable community, but I was fortunate enough to have a mother and a stepfather. My stepfather was my everything, and he had the ability to provide the bare necessities that were more than what many other kids in my neighborhood had. Still, it was not a life with bells and whistles. Due to this, all odds according to man were stacked against me just because of my zip code. According to statistics, I should have had my first child while I was in high school, had no more than one year of college, worked a job that paid minimum wage, and primarily dependent on government assistance. But because I am the child of the King, God moved every mountain that rose up against me. Because of His will for my life, I made it through high school without getting pregnant. I not only completed four years of college to achieve my Bachelor of Science in nursing, but I also obtained my Master of Science in nursing and am currently working on my doctorate of nursing practice. I make well above minimum wage, and I was fortunate to only have to receive government public assistance for a very brief period while I transitioned from nursing school to motherhood. Now, please do not misunderstand me: I have faced many challenges through all of my above accomplishments but because I am a child of the King my life is not easier, it is possible. While I know that we all have different backgrounds, some of you may have had it worse than me and some may have had it better than me, but the important point here is to know you are worthy and you are enough. Go after everything that God has for you, so that when your family and friends have their three minutes to describe your life, they can talk about the legacy you left behind as a human being, as a friend, as a contributor to the kingdom of God, and in the healthcare profession.

You are fully prepared.

I pray that you are equally empowered.

And through Christ, you are duly blessed. Arise and dominate as the salt and light of the earth. Seek God for your vision, and create your legacy *In Health, On Purpose!*

Sometimes The Smallest Step In The Right Direction Ends Up Being The Biggest Step Of Your Life. Tip Toe If You Must, But Take The Step----- Unknown

I pray this book has blessed you beyond measure and left you with a renewed outlook on your respective role as a healthcare professional. You now have a foundation in which you can build upon so that you can courageously, boldly, and unapologetically be "In Health, On Purpose!"

Moreover, to simply read and amen many of the sentiments of **"In Health, On Purpose! Awakening Your True Call In The Healthcare Profession"** is not enough. You MUST now be ABOUT ACTION. So in the next section of this book you will find journal sheets, discovery exercises, daily affirmation templates, and a 31-day "About Action" checklists, to assist you on your journey of becoming a purposeful and intentional healthcare professional.

These guides, worksheets, and checklist are designed for us to really and truly start that journey of discovering why we are in the healthcare profession and what is that pivotal contribution that God needs us to make to the profession. Now I want to warn you that some of the exercises and reflection moments will cause you to go beyond your role as a healthcare professional and tap into some personal things about yourself, but know that this is a necessary part of getting "In Health, On Purpose!"

I am here cheering you on every single step of the way!

Living Purposefully,
Nicole Thomas

70

Daily Affirmation

I WILL HEAR THE VOICE OF THE HOLY SPIRIT WITHIN ME

I AM THE HEAD AND NOT THE TAIL

I AM A LENDER AND NOT A BORROWER

I WILL LEAD AND NOT FOLLOW

I WILL CREATE AND NOT DESTROY

I SET NEW STANDARDS

I DEFY THE ODDS

I AM A LEADER

I AM ABOVE AND NOT BENEATH

I AM LOVED BY GOD

I AM CHOSEN BY GOD

I AM PROTECTED BY GOD

NO WEAPON FORMED AGAINST ME SHALL PROSPER

AND EVERY TONGUE THAT RISES UP AGAINST ME IN JUDGMENT SHALL BE CONDEMNED

I AM A CHAMPION AND

EVERYTHING I TOUCH TURNS TO GOLD

EVERYTHING I'M SEEKING IS NOW SEEKING ME

IT'S MY SEASON

IT'S MY TURN

I AM HUMBLE

I AM HAPPY

I AM STRONG

I WILL NEVER BE BROKE ANOTHER DAY IN MY LIFE

I AM WEALTHY

I AM A CHAMPION

I AM CREATED FOR GREATNESS

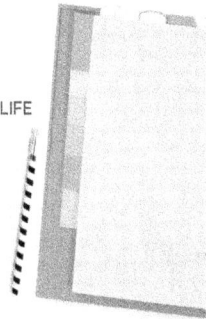

and so it is...

In Health, On Purpose!

It's Find Your Purpose
DISCOVERY JOURNAL

MY DAILY AFFIRMATIONS

LIST IN PRESENT TENSE

1 _____

2 _____

3 _____

4 _____

5 _____

6 _____

7 _____

8 _____

9 _____

10 _____

Let's Find Your Purpose
DISCOVERY JOURNAL

PURPOSE PRAYER

Dear God,

I thank you for traveling into my today and for being a present help.

I ask that you forgive me for all of my sins that I have committed knowingly and unknowingly.

Lord I ask that you continue to allow the holy spirit to speak to me to help me to conceive my purpose as a _____ (list your role as a healthcare professional) because a purposeful life is how I want to live my life so that I can magnify and glorify your name.

I know that finding my purpose will require me to give myself to you, for me to sit in stillness to allow you to speak to me through the holy spirit, and for me to go deep into places that I do not want to go into, but I am committed to living my life according to your will so I will patiently trust the process.

God when I get weary and tired with discovering my purpose as a _____ (list healthcare profession), I ask that you be my refuge and strength because I am reminded of your promise to me to come to you, all who are weary and burdened, and I will give you rest. Take my yoke upon you learn from me, for I am gentle and humble in heart, and you will find rest for your souls (Matthew 11:28-29).

Amen

It's Find Your Purpose DISCOVERY JOURNAL

PURPOSE PRAYER

Dear God,

I thank you for waking me up and giving me breath in my body!

I thank you for _____.

God as I begin my day, I ask that you give me the ability to drown out all the noise that surrounds me and allow the voice of the holy spirit to speak to me today.

God I want to live my life according to your will and not mine so that I can glorify you.

I ask that you give me clarity surrounding my purpose as a _____ (List current healthcare role) and once you provide that clarity and understanding surrounding my purpose as _____, I ask that you give me wisdom, courage, and the tenacity to walk purposefully.

God I know that walking in divine purpose is not about me, but to magnify your name so even when I do not initially understand, I promise to trust you.

In Proverbs 19:21 you declare that many are the plans in a person's heart, but it is the Lord's purpose that prevails.

I declare that the purpose in which you have called me to healthcare will prevail and I will walk boldly in MY purpose.

Amen

Let's Find Your Purpose DISCOVERY JOURNAL

EXERCISE

"To live your purpose, you have to dare to be even more of who you really are"

On your Google calendar schedule a meeting, lunch date, or dinner date with yourself (*no one else, just YOU!*) While at the meeting, on the lunch or dinner date, reflect, rate, and answer the following:

On a scale of 0-10 how alive do you feel at this present moment? (0 NOT ALIVE AT ALL - 10 ALL THE WAY ALIVE)

Based off of how you feel right now, list 3 things that would make you feel more alive right now?

1.
2.
3.

On a scale of 0-10 how alive do you feel as a healthcare professional at this present moment?
(0 NOT ALIVE AT ALL - 10 ALL THE WAY ALIVE)

Based on how you feel as a healthcare professional right now, list 3 things that would make you feel more alive as a healthcare professional right now?

1.
2.
3.

On a scale of 0-10 how motivated and inspired are you?
(0 NOT MOTIVATED & INSPIRED AT ALL - 10 TOTALLY MOTIVATED & INSPIRED)

Based on how motivated & inspired you are, identify 3 things that motivate and inspire you.

1.
2.
3.

On a scale of 0-10 how motivated and inspired are you as a healthcare professional?
(0 NOT MOTIVATED & INSPIRED AT ALL - 10 TOTALLY MOTIVATED & INSPIRED)

Based on how motivated & inspired you are as a healthcare professional, identify 3 things that motivate and inspire you to continue working as a healthcare professional.

1.
2.
3.

It's Find Your Purpose
DISCOVERY JOURNAL

EXERCISE

As a business standard all entrepreneurs and leaders have a business card that most likely identifies their company/organization, list their title and credentials, and identify the product or services that they offer. But what about a business card tha ONLY outlines your purpose to let everyone who you came into contact with to know your purpose. Now that you have been working for days, weeks, months, or years it is time to develop your "Purpose Card."

IN THIS EXERCISE WE ARE GOING TO DO THE FOLLOWING:

List your purpose by starting off with the phrase "The purpose of my work is to..." Complete the rest of this statement with what *YOUR* God given purpose is as a healthcare professional.

List the motto, scripture, or affirmation that you live by as a healthcare professional.

Identify symbols, pictures, or colors that inspires you.

Once this is completed head over to your local graphic designer, fiverr, or VistaPrint to have your "Purpose Card" created with the above information and whenever you are out networking, at a meeting or convention, at a interview, etc. pass out your "Purpose Card."

Don't forget to list your name, email, website, or contact number.

Let's Find Your Purpose
DISCOVERY JOURNAL

I want to discover my purpose as a healthcare provider because:

The things that brought me joy as a child were?

Before the world told me what my role as a healthcare provider would be, I loved the profession because:

What am I passionate about as a healthcare professional?

The things that I am doing as a healthcare professional and in my personal life that do not bring me joy and fulfillment include:

When it is all said and done, what matters the most to me as a human-being and a healthcare professional include:

Am I on track with what matters the most to me personally as a human-being and professionally as a healthcare professional?

It's Find Your Purpose
DISCOVERY JOURNAL

"The purpose of your life is to discover who you are. It is to meet yourself and to identify what you are made of and what you are made for."

During the past 30 days, the moments as a healthcare professional that have evoked feelings of joy, satisfaction, and purpose were:

_____
_____
_____
_____
_____
_____

During the last month, I came alive as a healthcare professional when:

_____
_____
_____
_____
_____

What were you doing? Who were you being?

5 to 10 of the most significant challenges that I have encountered as a healthcare professional include:

_____
_____
_____
_____

As I overcame these challenges I utilized the following talents and gifts:

_____
_____
_____
_____
_____

I thought of the following ideas to rectify these challenges:

_____
_____
_____
_____

I am inspired to continue working as a healthcare professional because:

_____
_____
_____
_____

Let's Find Your Purpose

DISCOVERY JOURNAL

DISCOVERY CHECKLIST

Date

Discovering One's "Purpose" in life essentially boils down to finding those one or two things that are bigger than yourself and bigger than those around you. And to find them you must get off your couch and act, and take the time to think beyond yourself, to think greater than yourself, and paradoxically, to image a world without yourself.
-Unknown

PRAYED

- ☐ MORNING PRAYER
- ☐ MORNING MEDITATION
- ☐ EVENING PRAYER
- ☐ EVENING MEDITATION

ONE THING I WILL DO TODAY THAT I LOVE:

TO TAKE CARE OF ME,
TODAY I MUST:

Brain Dump

Top 2 things that happened in my
day that brought me unhappiness:

_____

_____

TODAY'S WORD
THAT DESCRIBES ME AS A
HEALTHCARE PROFESSIONAL:

**TODAY'S TOP 3
SELF-REFLECTIONS**

1.

2.

3.

Today I'm Grateful For:

Let's Find Your Purpose
DISCOVERY JOURNAL

DISCOVERY CHECKLIST Date [   ]

You Only Live Once, but if you do it right, once is enough.
-Mae West

PRAYED
- ☐ MORNING PRAYER
- ☐ MORNING MEDITATION
- ☐ EVENING PRAYER
- ☐ EVENING MEDITATION

ONE THING I WILL DO TODAY THAT I LOVE:

TO TAKE CARE OF ME, TODAY I MUST:

Brain Dump

Top 2 things that happened in my day that brought me unhappiness:
_____
_____

TODAY'S WORD
THAT DESCRIBES ME AS A HEALTHCARE PROFESSIONAL:

TODAY'S TOP 3 SELF-REFLECTIONS
1.
2.
3.

Today I'm Grateful For:

Let's Find Your Purpose DISCOVERY JOURNAL

DISCOVERY CHECKLIST

Date [   ]

> The Real voyage of discovery consist not in seeking
> new landscape but in having new eyes.
> -Marcel Proust

PRAYED

☐ MORNING PRAYER
☐ MORNING MEDITATION
☐ EVENING PRAYER
☐ EVENING MEDITATION

ONE THING I WILL DO TODAY THAT I LOVE:

TO TAKE CARE OF ME.
TODAY I MUST:

Brain Dump

Top 2 things that happened in my
day that brought me unhappiness:

_____

_____

TODAY'S WORD
THAT DESCRIBES ME AS A
HEALTHCARE PROFESSIONAL:

**TODAY'S TOP 3
SELF-REFLECTIONS**

1.
2.
3.

Today I'm Grateful For:

It's Find Your Purpose
DISCOVERY JOURNAL

DISCOVERY CHECKLIST

Date [ ]

> If you can't figure out your purpose, figure out your passion, For your passion will lead you to your purpose.
> -Bishop T.D Jakes

PRAYED
- [ ] MORNING PRAYER
- [ ] MORNING MEDITATION
- [ ] EVENING PRAYER
- [ ] EVENING MEDITATION

ONE THING I WILL DO TODAY THAT I LOVE:

TO TAKE CARE OF ME, TODAY I MUST:

Brain Dump

Top 2 things that happened in my day that brought me unhappiness:
_____
_____

TODAY'S WORD
THAT DESCRIBES ME AS A HEALTHCARE PROFESSIONAL:

TODAY'S TOP 3 SELF-REFLECTIONS
1
2.
3

Today I'm Grateful For:

Let's Find Your Purpose
DISCOVERY JOURNAL

DISCOVERY CHECKLIST Date

Your work is to discover your work and then with
all your heart to give yourself to it.
–Buddah

PRAYED

- [ ] MORNING PRAYER
- [ ] MORNING MEDITATION
- [ ] EVENING PRAYER
- [ ] EVENING MEDITATION

ONE THING I WILL DO TODAY THAT I LOVE:

TO TAKE CARE OF ME,
TODAY I MUST:

Brain Dump

Top 2 things that happened in my
day that brought me unhappiness:

_____

_____

TODAY'S WORD
THAT DESCRIBES ME AS A
HEALTHCARE PROFESSIONAL:

**TODAY'S TOP 3
SELF-REFLECTIONS**

1.

2.

3.

Today I'm Grateful For:

Let's Find Your Purpose
DISCOVERY JOURNAL

DISCOVERY CHECKLIST

Date _____

> The two most important days in your life are the day you were
> born and the day you figure out why.
> —Mark Twain

PRAYED

- [ ] MORNING PRAYER
- [ ] MORNING MEDITATION
- [ ] EVENING PRAYER
- [ ] EVENING MEDITATION

ONE THING I WILL DO TODAY THAT I LOVE:

_____

TO TAKE CARE OF ME, TODAY I MUST:

Brain Dump

Top 2 things that happened in my day that brought me unhappiness:

_____

_____

TODAY'S WORD
THAT DESCRIBES ME AS A HEALTHCARE PROFESSIONAL:

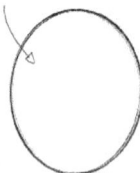

TODAY'S TOP 3 SELF-REFLECTIONS

1.
2.
3.

Today I'm Grateful For:

It's Find Your Purpose DISCOVERY JOURNAL

DISCOVERY CHECKLIST Date [   ]

Transformation is a process and as life happens there are tons of ups and
downs. It's a journey of discovery, there are moments on mountain
tops and moments in deep valleys of despair.
-Rick Warren

ONE THING I WILL DO TODAY THAT I LOVE:

PRAYED
- ☐ MORNING PRAYER
- ☐ MORNING MEDITATION
- ☐ EVENING PRAYER
- ☐ EVENING MEDITATION

TO TAKE CARE OF ME,
TODAY I MUST:

Brain Dump

Top 2 things that happened in my
day that brought me unhappiness:

_____

_____

**TODAY'S
WORD**
THAT DESCRIBES ME AS A
HEALTHCARE PROFESSIONAL:

**TODAY'S TOP 3
SELF-REFLECTIONS**

1
2:
3

Today I'm Grateful For:

Let's Find Your Purpose
DISCOVERY JOURNAL

DISCOVERY CHECKLIST Date [   ]

> If you want a happy life, tie it to a goal, not to people or things.
> -Albert Einstein

PRAYED
☐ **MORNING PRAYER**
☐ **MORNING MEDITATION**
☐ **EVENING PRAYER**
☐ **EVENING MEDITATION**

ONE THING I WILL DO TODAY THAT I LOVE:

TO TAKE CARE OF ME, TODAY I MUST:

Brain Dump

Top 2 things that happened in my day that brought me unhappiness:

_____

_____

TODAY'S WORD
THAT DESCRIBES ME AS A HEALTHCARE PROFESSIONAL:

TODAY'S TOP 3 SELF-REFLECTIONS
1.
2.
3.

Today I'm Grateful For:

It's Find Your Purpose
DISCOVERY JOURNAL

DISCOVERY CHECKLIST Date [   ]

> The best way to get rid of pain is to feel the pain. And when you feel the pain and go beyon it, you'll see there's a very intense love that is wanting to awaken itself.
> -Deepok Chopra

ONE THING I WILL DO TODAY THAT I LOVE:

PRAYED
- ☐ MORNING PRAYER
- ☐ MORNING MEDITATION
- ☐ EVENING PRAYER
- ☐ EVENING MEDITATION

TO TAKE CARE OF ME, TODAY I MUST:

Brain Dump

Top 2 things that happened in my day that brought me unhappiness:
_____
_____

TODAY'S WORD
THAT DESCRIBES ME AS A HEALTHCARE PROFESSIONAL:

TODAY'S TOP 3 SELF-REFLECTIONS

1
2
3

Today I'm Grateful For:

Let's Find Your Purpose
DISCOVERY JOURNAL

DISCOVERY CHECKLIST Date _____

Time is a created thing. To Say " I don't have time" is
like saying I don't want to.
-Lao Tzu

PRAYED
- [ ] MORNING PRAYER
- [ ] MORNING MEDITATION
- [ ] EVENING PRAYER
- [ ] EVENING MEDITATION

ONE THING I WILL DO TODAY THAT I LOVE:

TO TAKE CARE OF ME, TODAY I MUST:

Brain Dump

Top 2 things that happened in my day that brought me unhappiness:
_____
_____

TODAY'S WORD
THAT DESCRIBES ME AS A HEALTHCARE PROFESSIONAL:

TODAY'S TOP 3 SELF-REFLECTIONS
1.
2.
3.

Today I'm Grateful For:

Let's Find Your Purpose
DISCOVERY JOURNAL

DISCOVERY CHECKLIST
Date [   ]

You didn't come this far to only come this far. So go ahead and cry, but
let those tears water the seeds you are sowing.
-Nicole Thomas

PRAYED
- [ ] MORNING PRAYER
- [ ] MORNING MEDITATION
- [ ] EVENING PRAYER
- [ ] EVENING MEDITATION

ONE THING I WILL DO TODAY THAT I LOVE:

TO TAKE CARE OF ME,
TODAY I MUST:

Brain Dump

Top 2 things that happened in my
day that brought me unhappiness:
_____
_____

TODAY'S WORD
THAT DESCRIBES ME AS A
HEALTHCARE PROFESSIONAL:

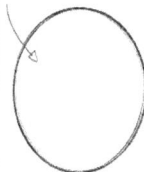

**TODAY'S TOP 3
SELF-REFLECTIONS**
1
2.
3

Today I'm Grateful For:

Let's Find Your Purpose
DISCOVERY JOURNAL

DISCOVERY CHECKLIST   Date [   ]

Good, Better, Best. Never let it rest. Til your good is better and your better
is best.
-St. Jerome

ONE THING I WILL DO TODAY THAT I LOVE:

PRAYED
- ☐ MORNING PRAYER
- ☐ MORNING MEDITATION
- ☐ EVENING PRAYER
- ☐ EVENING MEDITATION

TO TAKE CARE OF ME,
TODAY I MUST:

Brain Dump

Top 2 things that happened in my
day that brought me unhappiness:

_____

_____

TODAY'S WORD
THAT DESCRIBES ME AS A
HEALTHCARE PROFESSIONAL:

TODAY'S TOP 3 SELF-REFLECTIONS

1.
2.
3.

Today I'm Grateful For:

Let's Find Your Purpose
DISCOVERY JOURNAL

DISCOVERY CHECKLIST

Date _____

Don't watch the clock; do what it does. Keep Goin.
-Sam Levenson

PRAYED

- [ ] **MORNING PRAYER**
- [ ] **MORNING MEDITATION**
- [ ] **EVENING PRAYER**
- [ ] **EVENING MEDITATION**

ONE THING I WILL DO TODAY THAT I LOVE:

TO TAKE CARE OF ME,
TODAY I MUST:

Brain Dump

Top 2 things that happened in my
day that brought me unhappiness:
_____
_____

TODAY'S WORD
THAT DESCRIBES ME AS A
HEALTHCARE PROFESSIONAL:

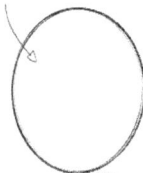

TODAY'S TOP 3 SELF-REFLECTIONS

1.
2.
3.

Today I'm Grateful For:

Let's Find Your Purpose
DISCOVERY JOURNAL

DISCOVERY CHECKLIST

Date [   ]

> Start where you are. Use what you have. Do what you can.
> -Authur Ashe

PRAYED
- [ ] MORNING PRAYER
- [ ] MORNING MEDITATION
- [ ] EVENING PRAYER
- [ ] EVENING MEDITATION

ONE THING I WILL DO TODAY THAT I LOVE:

TO TAKE CARE OF ME,
TODAY I MUST:

Brain Dump

Top 2 things that happened in my
day that brought me unhappiness:

_____

_____

TODAY'S
WORD
THAT DESCRIBES ME AS A
HEALTHCARE PROFESSIONAL:

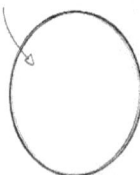

TODAY'S TOP 3
SELF-REFLECTIONS

1.

2.

3.

Today I'm Grateful For:

Let's Find Your Purpose
DISCOVERY JOURNAL

DISCOVERY CHECKLIST
Date

Know this one thing, God did not create you to simply exist in this life. He created you for a divine purpose that only you can fill. Discover that Purpose and live your life on that Purpose.
-Nicole Thomas

PRAYED
- ☐ MORNING PRAYER
- ☐ MORNING MEDITATION
- ☐ EVENING PRAYER
- ☐ EVENING MEDITATION

ONE THING I WILL DO TODAY THAT I LOVE:

TO TAKE CARE OF ME. TODAY I MUST:

Brain Dump

Top 2 things that happened in my day that brought me unhappiness:

TODAY'S WORD
THAT DESCRIBES ME AS A HEALTHCARE PROFESSIONAL:

TODAY'S TOP 3 SELF-REFLECTIONS
1.
2.
3.

Today I'm Grateful For:

Let's Find Your Purpose
DISCOVERY JOURNAL

DISCOVERY CHECKLIST

Date

> Passion Alone isn't enough. Combine that with faith, prayers, and hustle to make it happen.
> -Nicole Thomas

PRAYED

- ☐ MORNING PRAYER
- ☐ MORNING MEDITATION
- ☐ EVENING PRAYER
- ☐ EVENING MEDITATION

ONE THING I WILL DO TODAY THAT I LOVE:

TO TAKE CARE OF ME, TODAY I MUST:

Brain Dump

Top 2 things that happened in my day that brought me unhappiness:

_____

_____

TODAY'S WORD
THAT DESCRIBES ME AS A HEALTHCARE PROFESSIONAL:

TODAY'S TOP 3 SELF-REFLECTIONS

1.
2.
3.

Today I'm Grateful For:

Let's Find Your Purpose
DISCOVERY JOURNAL

DISCOVERY CHECKLIST

Date [ ]

This is a day that you have never seen before and you will never see again. So make it count.
-Nicole Thomas

PRAYED

- [ ] MORNING PRAYER
- [ ] MORNING MEDITATION
- [ ] EVENING PRAYER
- [ ] EVENING MEDITATION

ONE THING I WILL DO TODAY THAT I LOVE:

TO TAKE CARE OF ME, TODAY I MUST:

Brain Dump

Top 2 things that happened in my day that brought me unhappiness:

_____

_____

TODAY'S WORD
THAT DESCRIBES ME AS A HEALTHCARE PROFESSIONAL:

TODAY'S TOP 3 SELF-REFLECTIONS

1.

2.

3.

Today I'm Grateful For:

It's Find Your Purpose
DISCOVERY JOURNAL

DISCOVERY CHECKLIST

Date: _____

I may not be able to control my outcome, but I can surely control my outlook and its sky's the limit for me.
-Nicole Thomas

PRAYED
- [ ] MORNING PRAYER
- [ ] MORNING MEDITATION
- [ ] EVENING PRAYER
- [ ] EVENING MEDITATION

ONE THING I WILL DO TODAY THAT I LOVE:

_____

TO TAKE CARE OF ME, TODAY I MUST:

Brain Dump

Top 2 things that happened in my day that brought me unhappiness:

_____

_____

TODAY'S WORD
THAT DESCRIBES ME AS A HEALTHCARE PROFESSIONAL:

TODAY'S TOP 3 SELF-REFLECTIONS
1.
2.
3.

Today I'm Grateful For:

Let's Find Your Purpose
DISCOVERY JOURNAL

DISCOVERY CHECKLIST

Date

> Follow your dreams. I am not saying it's going to be easy, but
> I am saying it's going to be worth it.
> -Machingura

PRAYED

- [ ] MORNING PRAYER
- [ ] MORNING MEDITATION
- [ ] EVENING PRAYER
- [ ] EVENING MEDITATION

ONE THING I WILL DO TODAY THAT I LOVE:

TO TAKE CARE OF ME,
TODAY I MUST:

Brain Dump

Top 2 things that happened in my
day that brought me unhappiness:

_____

_____

**TODAY'S
WORD**
THAT DESCRIBES ME AS A
HEALTHCARE PROFESSIONAL:

**TODAY'S TOP 3
SELF-REFLECTIONS**

1.

2.

3.

Today I'm Grateful For:

It's Find Your Purpose
DISCOVERY JOURNAL

DISCOVERY CHECKLIST

Date: _____

> Before the plan, there is an idea. Before the idea, there is a purpose. Before the purpose, there is your spirit... aching to express itself.
> —Paresh Shah

PRAYED
- [ ] MORNING PRAYER
- [ ] MORNING MEDITATION
- [ ] EVENING PRAYER
- [ ] EVENING MEDITATION

ONE THING I WILL DO TODAY THAT I LOVE:

_____

TO TAKE CARE OF ME, TODAY I MUST:

Brain Dump

Top 2 things that happened in my day that brought me unhappiness:

_____

_____

TODAY'S WORD THAT DESCRIBES ME AS A HEALTHCARE PROFESSIONAL:

TODAY'S TOP 3 SELF-REFLECTIONS

1.
2.
3.

Today I'm Grateful For:

Let's Find Your Purpose DISCOVERY JOURNAL

DISCOVERY CHECKLIST

Date

> Courage is not the absence of fear, but the triumph over it.
> -Nelson Mandela

PRAYED

- [ ] MORNING PRAYER
- [ ] MORNING MEDITATION
- [ ] EVENING PRAYER
- [ ] EVENING MEDITATION

ONE THING I WILL DO TODAY THAT I LOVE:

TO TAKE CARE OF ME,
TODAY I MUST:

Brain Dump

Top 2 things that happened in my day that brought me unhappiness:

_____

_____

TODAY'S WORD
THAT DESCRIBES ME AS A
HEALTHCARE PROFESSIONAL:

TODAY'S TOP 3 SELF-REFLECTIONS

1.

2.

3.

Today I'm Grateful For:

Let's Find Your Purpose
DISCOVERY JOURNAL

DISCOVERY CHECKLIST

Date [   ]

> You don't get in life what you want; you get in life what you are.
> -Les Brown

PRAYED
- [ ] MORNING PRAYER
- [ ] MORNING MEDITATION
- [ ] EVENING PRAYER
- [ ] EVENING MEDITATION

ONE THING I WILL DO TODAY THAT I LOVE:

TO TAKE CARE OF ME, TODAY I MUST:

Brain Dump

Top 2 things that happened in my day that brought me unhappiness:

_____

_____

TODAY'S WORD
THAT DESCRIBES ME AS A HEALTHCARE PROFESSIONAL:

TODAY'S TOP 3 SELF-REFLECTIONS
1.
2.
3.

Today I'm Grateful For:

Let's Find Your Purpose
DISCOVERY JOURNAL

DISCOVERY CHECKLIST

Date

If you don't build your dreams, someone else will hire
you to build theirs.
-Tony Gaskins

PRAYED

☐ MORNING PRAYER
☐ MORNING MEDITATION
☐ EVENING PRAYER
☐ EVENING MEDITATION

ONE THING I WILL DO TODAY THAT I LOVE:

TO TAKE CARE OF ME,
TODAY I MUST:

Brain Dump

Top 2 things that happened in my
day that brought me unhappiness:

_____

_____

**TODAY'S
WORD**
THAT DESCRIBES ME AS A
HEALTHCARE PROFESSIONAL:

**TODAY'S TOP 3
SELF-REFLECTIONS**

1.

2.

3.

Today I'm Grateful For:

It's Find Your Purpose
DISCOVERY JOURNAL

DISCOVERY CHECKLIST   Date [_____]

Never give up on a dream just because of the time it will take to accomplish it.
The time will pass anyway.
-Earl Nightingale

PRAYED
- ☐ MORNING PRAYER
- ☐ MORNING MEDITATION
- ☐ EVENING PRAYER
- ☐ EVENING MEDITATION

ONE THING I WILL DO TODAY THAT I LOVE:

_____

TO TAKE CARE OF ME,
TODAY I MUST:

Brain Dump

Top 2 things that happened in my
day that brought me unhappiness:

_____

_____

TODAY'S WORD
THAT DESCRIBES ME AS A
HEALTHCARE PROFESSIONAL:

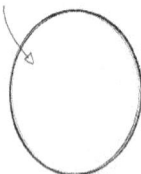

TODAY'S TOP 3 SELF-REFLECTIONS

1
2
3

Today I'm Grateful For:

Let's Find Your Purpose
DISCOVERY JOURNAL

DISCOVERY CHECKLIST Date [   ]

66

to accomplish it. The time will pass anyway. --- Earl Nightingale

PRAYED
- [ ] MORNING PRAYER
- [ ] MORNING MEDITATION
- [ ] EVENING PRAYER
- [ ] EVENING MEDITATION

ONE THING I WILL DO TODAY THAT I LOVE:

TO TAKE CARE OF ME,
TODAY I MUST:

Brain Dump

Top 2 things that happened in my
day that brought me unhappiness:

TODAY'S WORD
THAT DESCRIBES ME AS A
HEALTHCARE PROFESSIONAL:

TODAY'S TOP 3
SELF-REFLECTIONS

1.
2.
3.

Today I'm Grateful For:

It's Find Your Purpose
DISCOVERY JOURNAL

DISCOVERY CHECKLIST
Date

> I don't stop when I am tired, I stop when I am done.
> -James Bond

PRAYED
- ☐ MORNING PRAYER
- ☐ MORNING MEDITATION
- ☐ EVENING PRAYER
- ☐ EVENING MEDITATION

ONE THING I WILL DO TODAY THAT I LOVE:

TO TAKE CARE OF ME, TODAY I MUST:

Brain Dump

Top 2 things that happened in my day that brought me unhappiness:

_____

_____

TODAY'S WORD THAT DESCRIBES ME AS A HEALTHCARE PROFESSIONAL:

TODAY'S TOP 3 SELF-REFLECTIONS
1.
2.
3.

Today I'm Grateful For:

It's Find Your Purpose DISCOVERY JOURNAL

DISCOVERY CHECKLIST Date [   ]

If your dreams don't scare you, they aren't big enough.
-Muhammad Ali

PRAYED

- [ ] MORNING PRAYER
- [ ] MORNING MEDITATION
- [ ] EVENING PRAYER
- [ ] EVENING MEDITATION

ONE THING I WILL DO TODAY THAT I LOVE:

TO TAKE CARE OF ME,
TODAY I MUST:

Brain Dump

Top 2 things that happened in my
day that brought me unhappiness:

_____

_____

TODAY'S WORD
THAT DESCRIBES ME AS A
HEALTHCARE PROFESSIONAL:

**TODAY'S TOP 3
SELF-REFLECTIONS**

1.

2.

3.

Today I'm Grateful For:

It's Find Your Purpose
DISCOVERY JOURNAL

DISCOVERY CHECKLIST

Date [ ]

> I've failed over and over and over in my life.
> That's why I succeed.
> -Michael Jordan

PRAYED
- [ ] MORNING PRAYER
- [ ] MORNING MEDITATION
- [ ] EVENING PRAYER
- [ ] EVENING MEDITATION

ONE THING I WILL DO TODAY THAT I LOVE:

_____

TO TAKE CARE OF ME, TODAY I MUST:

Brain Dump

Top 2 things that happened in my day that brought me unhappiness:

_____

_____

TODAY'S WORD
THAT DESCRIBES ME AS A HEALTHCARE PROFESSIONAL:

TODAY'S TOP 3 SELF-REFLECTIONS

1

2:

3

Today I'm Grateful For:

DISCOVERY JOURNAL

DISCOVERY CHECKLIST

Date

> It took me 17 years and 114 days to become an overnight success.
> -Naomi Mosca

PRAYED
- [ ] MORNING PRAYER
- [ ] MORNING MEDITATION
- [ ] EVENING PRAYER
- [ ] EVENING MEDITATION

ONE THING I WILL DO TODAY THAT I LOVE:

TO GIVE MY LIFE TO ME, TODAY I MUST:

Brain Dump

Top 23 things that happened in my day that brought me true happiness:

TODAY'S WORD
THAT DESCRIBES ME AS A HEALTHCARE PROFESSIONAL

TODAY'S TOP 3 SELF-REFLECTIONS
1.
2.
3.

Today I'm Grateful For

Let's Find Your Purpose
DISCOVERY JOURNAL

DISCOVERY CHECKLIST

Date

> Today I will do what others wont, so tomorrow I can accomplish what others can't.
> ~Jerry Rice

ONE THING I WILL DO TODAY THAT I LOVE:

PRAYED
- [ ] MORNING PRAYER
- [ ] MORNING MEDITATION
- [ ] EVENING PRAYER
- [ ] EVENING MEDITATION

TO TAKE CARE OF ME, TODAY I MUST:

Brain Dump

Top 2 things that happened in my day that brought me unhappiness:
_____
_____

TODAY'S WORD THAT DESCRIBES ME AS A HEALTHCARE PROFESSIONAL:

TODAY'S TOP 3 SELF-REFLECTIONS
1.
2.
3.

Today I'm Grateful For:

Let's Find Your Purpose
DISCOVERY JOURNAL

DISCOVERY CHECKLIST
Date

In order to manifest your dream, you can't keep telling yourself how big the problem is, instead tell your problem how big your God is.
-Nicole Thomas

PRAYED
- [ ] MORNING PRAYER
- [ ] MORNING MEDITATION
- [ ] EVENING PRAYER
- [ ] EVENING MEDITATION

ONE THING I WILL DO TODAY THAT I LOVE:

TO TAKE CARE OF ME, TODAY I MUST:

Brain Dump

Top 2 things that happened in my day that brought me unhappiness:

TODAY'S WORD
THAT DESCRIBES ME AS A HEALTHCARE PROFESSIONAL:

TODAY'S TOP 3 SELF-REFLECTIONS
1.
2.
3.

Today I'm Grateful For:

Let's Find Your Purpose
DISCOVERY JOURNAL

DISCOVERY CHECKLIST

Date

I am who I say I am, I am who God says I am, I am In Health on Purpose!
-Nicole Thomas

PRAYED

- [ ] MORNING PRAYER
- [ ] MORNING MEDITATION
- [ ] EVENING PRAYER
- [ ] EVENING MEDITATION

ONE THING I WILL DO TODAY THAT I LOVE:

TO TAKE CARE OF ME, TODAY I MUST:

Brain Dump

Top 2 things that happened in my day that brought me unhappiness:

_____

_____

TODAY'S WORD
THAT DESCRIBES ME AS A HEALTHCARE PROFESSIONAL:

TODAY'S TOP 3 SELF-REFLECTIONS

1.
2.
3.

Today I'm Grateful For:

About the Author

• •

Nicole Thomas, RN, MSN, CCM, LNC, the founder of Nicole Thomas INC., an educational and empowerment firm that helps female healthcare professionals awaken to their God-given purpose in the health industry. She provides guidance, resources, and innovative solutions to help healthcare professionals create strategies and experience peace, inner joy and purpose.

As an experienced leader, Nicole has been a healthcare manager; associate director for Fortune 500 companies; and a supervisor to a team of nurses, nurse practitioners, and allied health professionals. She challenged her past employees to go deeper than their "job" roles in order to perform with purpose. Under Nicole's leadership and guidance, her personnel have furthered their education, advanced into higher roles and started their own businesses. As a stand-out leader, Nicole was awarded the Super Hero award, a prestigious honor given to only 125 professionals (out of the 1,500 nominated).

Nicole is also the owner of Impact Nurse Consulting and the president of Black Nurses Rock-Baton Rouge Chapter, a non-profit organization.

She is a devoted wife, mother of two beautiful girls,

sister, loyal friend, community health advocate, teacher, motivator, and action-oriented inspirational enthusiast.